Saint Lucia

Saint Lucia
Helen of the West Indies
FOURTH EDITION

Guy Ellis

MACMILLAN
CARIBBEAN

Macmillan Education
Between Towns Road, Oxford OX4 3PP
A division of Macmillan Publishers Limited
Companies and representatives throughout the world

www.macmillan-caribbean.com

ISBN-13: 978-1-4050-6645-7
ISBN-10: 1-4050-6645-8

First published 1986
Second Edition 1988
Third Edition 1994
This Edition 2006

Designed by Amanda Easter
Cover design by Gary Fielder
Layout by Melissa Orrom Swan

Cover photographs: all by Donald Nausbaum except bottom left and right
Chris Huxley, centre left Jenny Palmer.

The author and publishers would like to thank the following for permission to
use their photographs:
Donald Nausbaum: pp. i, ii, 2, 8, 10-11, 15, 18, 21, 31, 32, 44-5, 46, 47, 49,
   50-1, 53, 60, 63, 66, 73, 78-9, 86, 87, 92
Chris Huxley: pp. 4, 5, 16-17, 23, 55, 56, 57, 58-9, 69, 71, 72, 81, 82, 83, 84, 85
Jenny Palmer: pp. 27, 29, 30, 33, 36-7, 38-9, 42, 43, 48, 74, 75, 76, 77, 89, 90,
   91, 95
Art Directors & Trip: p.6
Corbis: p.41

Printed in Thailand

2010 2009 2008 2007 2006
10 9 8 7 6 5 4 3 2 1

Contents

Maps

Acknowledgements

The author and publishers wish to acknowledge, with thanks, the following photographic sources:
Saint Lucia Tourist Board

The publishers have made every effort to trace the copyright holders, but if they have inadvertently overlooked any, they will be pleased to make the necessary arrangements at the first opportunity.

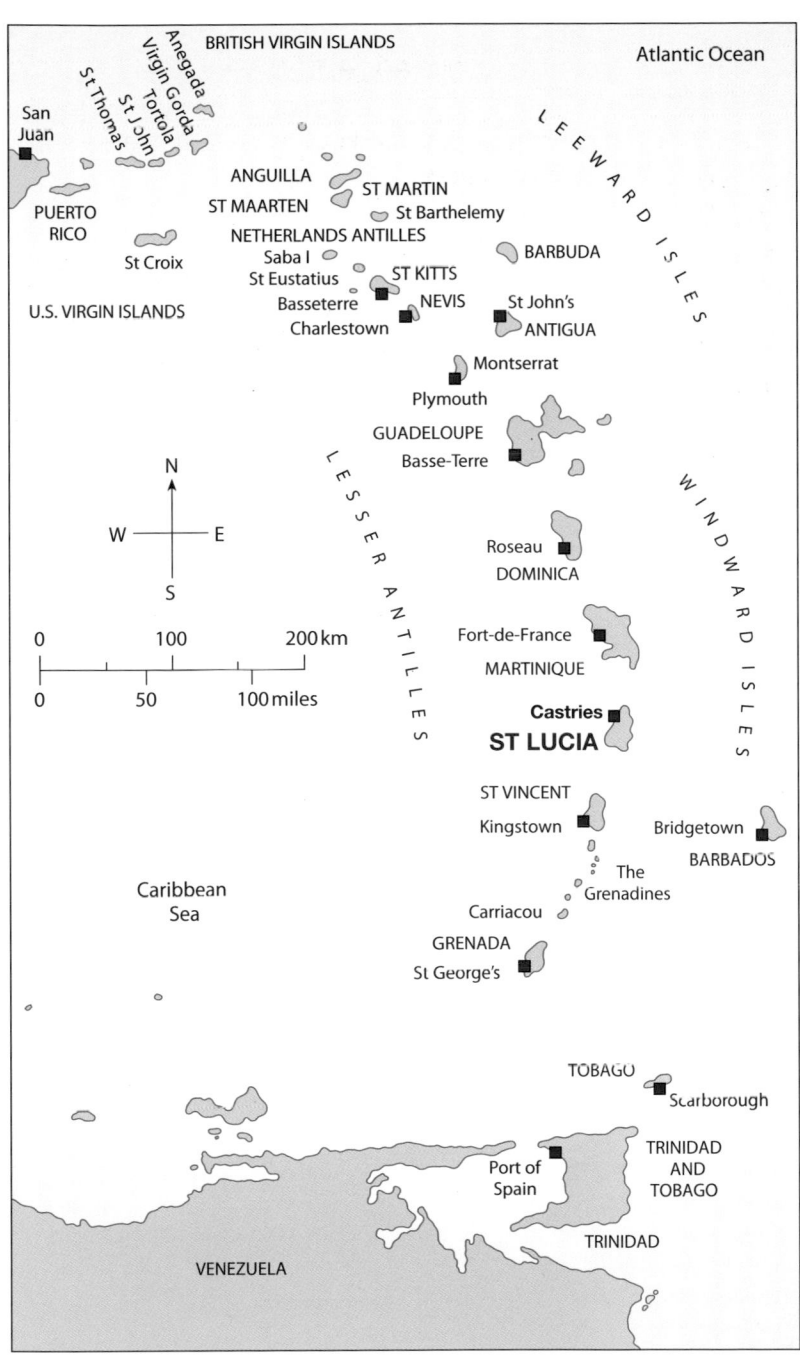

▲ The Eastern Caribbean

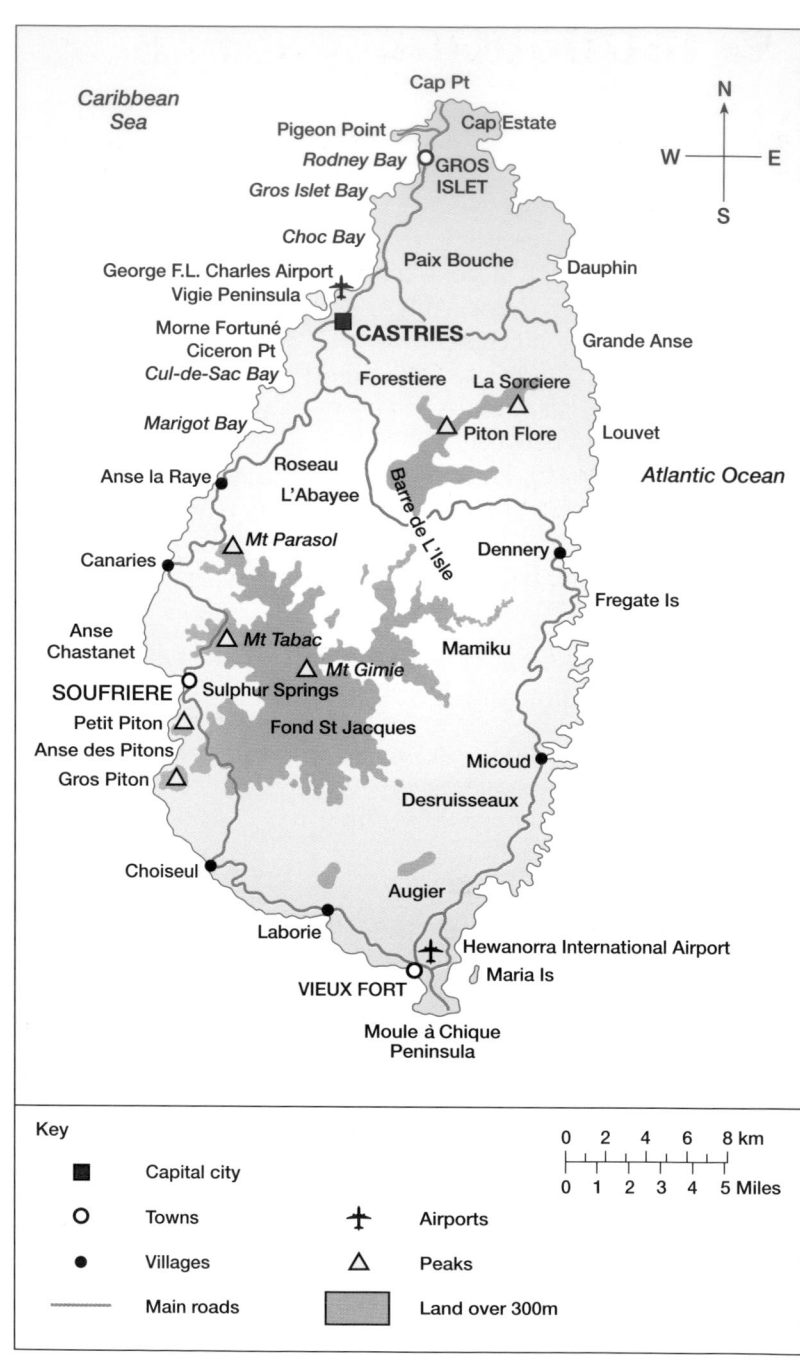

Saint Lucia

① Introducing Saint Lucia

Saint Lucia, an island of breathtaking beauty, birthplace of the French Empress Josephine and home of the only 'drive-in' volcano in the world, is located 90 miles (145 kilometres) north-west of Barbados, about 2600 miles (4000 km) from New York and 4200 miles (6700 km) from London. It is one of the volcanic islands of the West Indies that comprise the Lesser Antilles. Within this chain of islands, it belongs to the Windward Group, where it is second in size only to the Commonwealth of Dominica. Saint Lucia's 238 square miles (616 square km) make it nearly one-and-a-half times the size of Barbados. More precisely, it lies between the French island of Martinique to the north and St Vincent to the south, between 600° 53' and 610° 05' longitude west and 130° 43' and 140° 05' latitude north.

There was a time when Saint Lucia was referred to – often in somewhat disparaging terms – as 'a tiny dot on the map', despite its frequent appearance in the history books. Today, while this definition remains true in a geographic sense, Saint Lucia's image and status in the international arena has increased considerably. On the one hand, this rugged mountainous island was once a leading exporter of bananas among the Commonwealth islands of the Caribbean; although it is still in the business, production levels have fallen away drastically in recent years mainly due to a combination of domestic and foreign market factors. Tourism has taken over as the major engine of the economy, giving the island added prominence because of its emergence as a popular tourist destination. Hence, agriculture and tourism now form the backbone of the economy. But Saint Lucia is also famous as the only country of its size in the world to have produced two Nobel Prize winners – and within a short time span of thirteen years. It is now also the venue of one of the most successful jazz festivals in the world, held annually in the month of May.

The thick green forests of the hills and mountains of Saint Lucia contrast dramatically with the blue Atlantic on the east coast, and the tranquil turquoise Caribbean on the west. Miles and miles of white-sand beaches stretch along its coastline, lapped by incredibly translucent waters. Brilliant blue skies with snowy clouds and the ever-present warm Caribbean sunshine interspersed with occasional rainbow-coloured showers provide the serenity that most visitors seek. And yet, for nearly two centuries Saint Lucia was the object of some of the most bitter and hotly contested battles that raged in this

▲ French architecture, Soufriere

part of the world. During that time, the island changed hands between Britain and France a record fourteen times. This fact, plus its outstanding beauty, has earned Saint Lucia the title of 'Helen of the West Indies'.

Saint Lucia thus enjoys a dual heritage, and evidence of these frequent changes of ownership are still obvious: although English is the official language, a French-based Creole (Kweyol) is also spoken; the island's cuisine reflects both British and French influences; and also in its culture, folklore, religion, architecture and place names, Saint Lucia's strong French associations are evident everywhere on the island.

Saint Lucia's colourful history is further mirrored in the name changes which it has undergone over the centuries. As might be expected, the different designations have led to many spelling variations. According to some sources, the first name given to Saint Lucia was Amerindian in origin, this was 'Iouanalao', which means 'there where the iguana is found'. Later it was known as 'Hiwanarau', and later still as 'Hewanorra'. The first recorded use of the name 'Saint Lucia' came as late as the latter part of the sixteenth century. The name was given then as 'Saint Lucia', as it is today. A globe in the Vatican dated 1520 refers to an island of 'Saint Lucia', and in several French nautical documents of the early seventeenth century the name 'Sainte Alouzie' appears, followed some forty years later by 'Saint Alousie'.

Saint Lucia is an island best approached, perhaps, from the sea. Indeed, for hundreds of years, sailors of all nationalities must have made use of its spectacular mountain peaks to the south-western side to guide them to port. The main ridge of mountains runs almost through the entire 27-mile length of the island. Mount Gimie (3145 feet/959 metres (m) is the highest peak, but many others range between 2000 and 3000 feet (610–914 m). None, however, approaches the majesty of the twin peaks, Gros Piton (2619 feet/798 m) and Petit Piton (2461 feet/750 m), which rise sheer out of the Caribbean, near the south-western town of Soufriere. Every year thousands of visitors are drawn to Saint Lucia by the towering Pitons, now a national landmark, and the bubbling Sulphur Springs, not far away, formed by volcanic activity many centuries ago. From the Barre de L'Isle ridge of mountains many small rivers flow down to the magnificent shoreline.

Apart from the capital city of Castries – which boasts the most naturally sheltered harbour in the entire Caribbean – there are three other main towns: Soufriere, Vieux Fort on the southern tip and Gros Islet to the north. Six villages are strung out along the coast, bearing such French names as Anse la Raye, Canaries, Choiseul, Laborie, Micoud and Dennery. Over the last quarter century, several ecclesiastical parishes have been created, but these are mainly inland. The majority of the population is concentrated between Castries, the seat of government, and Gros Islet.

At one time, the main agricultural occupation here was sugarcane, then it became bananas or 'green gold' as the fruit was once commonly referred to. Coconuts and cocoa have declined in prominence. The island has become a new entrant into the financial services market as new avenues to generate economic activity are sought.

Now that growth and development are increasing in Saint Lucia, now that the islanders have become more 'progressive', many of their traditional customs have been swept out of sight, or confined to rural districts. But there are many Saint Lucians today working, often under the wary eye of the younger generation, for the retention of those customs and folk festivals that have their roots in both Africa and Western Europe and which are indeed a colourful and exciting part of the island's cultural heritage. Among the rural folk, only vestiges

▲ La Rose Flower Festival

remain today of the original Haitian-type voodoo. But folk dances like the Belair, Konte, Katumba and Solo, all inherited from the days of slavery, are still performed. La Rose and La Marguerite, in August and October respectively, are two rival flower festivals that have long been part of the island's folk culture. Their origins are obscure, but they have a political character, seen in references to English and French Republicans and Bonapartists. After the struggle between France and England had ceased, the rivalry between the two groups lost its political nature.

Activities of both festivals today include religious services, parades, a royal court, feasting and much dancing. Kele, a voodoo-type African ceremony that dates back over a hundred years, involves the sacrificing of a sheep. Whereas in earlier times the Roman Catholic Church frowned on this ritual, today attempts are being made to retain it as a key element of Saint Lucian folk culture. The biggest festival, however, is Carnival – two days of carefree merriment now moved to July from the pre-Lenten period before Ash Wednesday. On National Day (13 December) and at Christmas and New Year, some of Saint Lucia's oldest and most popular traditions come alive. A recent addition to the cultural calendar, and one which has become extremely popular is Jounen Kweyol (Creole Day) in October when

▲ Dunstan St Omer

huge open-air fairs are held to highlight Saint Lucia's rich and diverse folk culture and exhibit some of the old traditions that have been largely overtaken by modernization.

On a more modern level, in the fields of art, drama and literature, several Saint Lucians have risen to international prominence. By far the most widely acclaimed is playwright and poet Derek Walcott, who won the 1992 Nobel Prize for Literature. In the 1950s, Walcott and his twin brother, Roderick, now deceased, spearheaded the now defunct Saint Lucia Arts Guild. They enriched Saint Lucia's cultural life with a succession of outstanding plays, including *The Sea at Dauphin* and *Ti Jean and his Brothers*, which were staged as part of an annual arts festival. The works of artist Dunstan St Omer, who designed the Saint Lucia flag, his poet brother, Garth, playwright Stanley French and the poets John Robert Lee, Kendel Hippolyte and his wife, Jane, have also been widely acclaimed. One of Dunstan St Omer's greatest works is a mural which adorns the altar of a rural church at Jacmel, a few miles from Castries. Another prominent and popular personality

◀ Arthur Lewis

SIR WILLIAM ARTHUR LEWIS
BORN IN ST.LUCIA JANUARY 23, 1915
NOBEL PRIZE
FOR ECONOMICS - 1979
"A country without the Arts

in this field is the actor George 'Fish' Alphonse, who is also a member of the widely acclaimed Lapo Kabwit (Goat Skin), a group of mainly drummers who combine rhythm and poetry in a unique style of commentary on some of the social and other conditions of the day. Alphonse has also taken his solo stage performances overseas, including the UK, with great success.

The island's rich folk music, after an initial burst of enthusiasm in the 1970s when two outstanding groups, the Helenites and the Hewanorra Voices, and Frank Norville, put some of its most popular folk tunes on long-playing albums, has hit a low spot recently, but a revival is to be hoped for in the not-too-distant future, as music of all kinds is such an important aspect of Caribbean life. The annual Minvielle and Chastanet Fine Arts Exhibition provides those involved in the arts with an opportunity to compete with their peers for prominence and cash, with a number of prizes at stake in Literary, Performing and Visual categories.

As a further indication of Saint Lucia's determination to keep abreast of modern development, it offers, despite its small size, more than adequate news coverage, which ensures that the visitor is not cut off from the rest of the world while holidaying. *The Voice*, the oldest newspaper in the Eastern Caribbean, having been inaugurated in 1885, is published three times weekly, on Tuesdays, Thursdays and at weekends. There are also a number of other newspapers including *The Star* (thrice weekly) and the *St Lucia Mirror*, *The Crusader* and *One Caribbean*, which appear at weekends. The Roman Catholic Church publishes *The Chronicle* every month. There are six radio stations – Radio Saint Lucia, Radio Caribbean International, Helen FM, The Wave, Rhythm FM and Hot FM – and two television stations, all offering a variety of programmes. The TV stations relay mainly satellite programmes beamed from the United States. There are also two cable systems, one operated by the British multi-national Cable and Wireless and the other by a local concern, Cox Radio and Cable.

Despite its small size, Saint Lucia has produced a host of outstanding sons, many of whom have made their mark on the international scene as well. Easily the greatest achievers to date are the renowned economist and scholar Sir Arthur Lewis who, in 1979, won acclaim as the first West Indian to receive a Nobel Prize, capturing the prize for Economics, and the writer Derek Walcott. Both have been decorated with the island's highest honour, the Saint Lucia Cross, and declared national heroes.

The casual tourist, visiting for the very first time, may well unknowingly fail to take full advantage of a stimulating experience

▲ Derek Walcott

that is Saint Lucia both in its modern and traditional aspects. But armed with the right information, he or she can expect to enjoy the experience of a lifetime, for beneath Saint Lucia's serenity lies one of the most fascinating and romantic of the sunny Caribbean islands.

❷ Welcome 'home'

In a region where countries frequently boast of the hospitality of their people, Saint Lucians claim, with some justification as many visitors will tell you, to be at the top of the list. Over the years, visitors have paid glowing tribute to the easy-going, warm and instant friendliness of the islanders. It is the sort of compliment that has made this little island something of a 'home away from home' to the visitor, a slogan used by many hotels and guest houses in Saint Lucia to illustrate, sincerely, the level of their hospitality.

Warm smiles, friendly faces and a willingness to help are among the main characteristics of the Saint Lucian hospitality that has now become internationally famous. But that does not mean Saint Lucians should be taken for granted. In fact, the Saint Lucia Tourist Board offers a word of caution to the visitor in one of its pieces of promotional literature:

> We invite you to share in the beauty of our island and we offer you our hospitality. You will certainly find most things about us and our country new, exciting … some perhaps difficult to identify with. Please remember that though our history, culture and way of life differ almost entirely from your own, we offer it all for you to explore and enjoy. In return we crave your consideration when dealing with our people. Saint Lucians are, generally, warm friendly people who are worthy of your respect. We would like your visit with us to be a worthwhile and mutually enjoyable exchange between gracious visitor and hospitable hosts.

With the prospect of such a welcome, the question 'How do you get there?' automatically follows. Access to Saint Lucia is by both air and sea. Of course a few formalities are required to visit Saint Lucia. All foreigners wishing to visit the island must have passports unless they are British, Canadian or USA citizens possessing valid return tickets and some form of identity document. This group of visitors do not require visas but other nationals do.

From the air, Saint Lucia is indeed a sight to behold. First-time visitors, and regulars too, will be captivated by the sheer beauty of the lush, still unspoilt island, a dark-green leaf floating in the brilliant blue Caribbean.

Air Jamaica, British West Indian Airways, American Airlines, US Air and Air Canada operate scheduled flights between Saint Lucia and

North America. British Airways and Virgin Atlantic ferry visitors from Europe. A number of North American and European charter companies also fly to the island regularly. Between Saint Lucia and the rest of the Caribbean, Leeward Islands Air Transport (LIAT), Caribbean Star, Air Caraibes and Air Martinique provide useful services bringing in passengers from the neighbouring islands.

Saint Lucia has two commercial airports. Every year, the international airlines bring thousands of visitors to the island, landing them either at Hewanorra Airport at Vieux Fort, in the south and some 33 miles away from Castries, or at George F.L. Charles Airport (formerly known as Vigie and renamed after the island's first Chief Minister), just a few minutes' drive from the city. Hewanorra is a former United States base built during the Second World War and upgraded to full international standards, so that now it handles long-

range jet traffic. Its 9000-foot (2743 m) runway is one of the longest in the region. George F.L.Charles caters mainly for lighter planes. Both airports are suitably equipped for night landings. Outgoing travellers pay a tax at the airports. This is fixed at 35 Eastern Caribbean dollars (EC$) per person for travellers to the Caribbean Community region, and EC$54 for those leaving for other destinations.

The coastal configuration of Saint Lucia offers several potential deepwater ports and the island is thus fortunate, in spite of its limited area and small population, to possess two multi-functional ports at Castries and Vieux Fort, with further possibilities at Soufriere. There is also a harbour at Cul-de-Sac, used by the Hess Oil Terminal and other ports of entry at Marigot and Rodney Bay.

▼ Castries cruise ships

The Castries and Vieux Fort ports provide a broad spectrum of functions. Facilities exist for berthing, loading and unloading, cargo storage, the handling of unitized general cargo on pallets and in containers, and for trans-shipment. Port Castries is the more developed of the two ports. The ports of Castries and Vieux Fort together handle more than 400 000 tonnes of cargo annually. Both ports have been expanded and upgraded in recent years. The historic Port Castries is quietly building a reputation for quick and efficient handling of trans-shipment cargo at a reasonable cost.

As many as 200 cruise-ship calls are made to Saint Lucia every year. In fact, the cruise-ship tourist has become such an important factor in the island's overall tourism drive that exclusive facilities for this category of visitor have been provided at Pointe Seraphine in Castries harbour. These include docks for berthing, restaurants, duty-free shopping, the sale of local handicrafts and souvenirs and, of course, an information centre and entertainment area where local groups perform for visitors. Cruise-ship traffic to the island provides significant economic activity. Most important, though, is that each cruise-ship passenger is a potential long-staying visitor. The Saint Lucian community with its propensity to be gracious, warm and friendly, is always ready to welcome sea visitors.

Some 400 000 visitors arrive in the Castries port every year, many of them coming in on some of the largest passenger ships afloat. The port can now accommodate six large cruise ships at any one time. Carnival, Cunard, Sun Cruises, Renaissance, Celebrity, Royal Caribbean and Costa are among the cruise lines calling regularly at Castries.

From Saint Lucia, communication with the rest of the world is something of a dream. The island enjoys a state-of-the-art telecommunications with telephone, fax and telex and has an efficient postal service, not to mention several courier services. There is direct dialling to anywhere in the world. Cable and Wireless dominated the sector until recently when it was thrown open to competition. Today, another company, Digicel of Ireland, has established itself on the island. Both companies operate mobile telephone systems.

The main currency in use is the Eastern Caribbean dollar which has been stable since 1976, pegged to the United States dollar at the rate of US$1.00=EC$2.70. There are several foreign banks on the island, including the Royal Bank of Canada, Bank of Nova Scotia, Royal Bank of Trinidad and Tobago, First Caribbean International Bank (a merger of Barclays and Canadian Imperial Bank of Commerce). There is also an indigenous bank, 1st National Bank, which is more than sixty years old, and Bank of St Lucia. Banking hours are from 8.00 a.m. to 2.00 p.m. Mondays to Thursdays and 8.00 a.m. to 3.00 p.m. on Fridays, and all banks have Automatic Teller Machines (ATMs). Credit cards are widely accepted.

The Saint Lucia Tourist Board has set up information services at both airports. It is at these points, in fact, that the Saint Lucian friendliness and hospitality begins to assert itself. It is here that the visitor begins to feel as though he has never left home. There could be some differences, however, like the weather. Since Saint Lucia is a mere 14 degrees north of the equator, temperatures are tropical almost year-round with constant north-east trade winds. December to February are the coolest months, with temperatures ranging between 70° and 80° Fahrenheit (21–27°C). The rest of the year, look for 80° to 90° (27–32°C) temperatures. If you are thinking of settling in Saint Lucia, there are several real estate agencies that can assist. Some of the prime areas for residential housing are at Cap Estate, Marigot Bay, Bonne Terre and Rodney Bay.

③ Saint Lucia's history

The first settlers on Saint Lucia were the peaceful Arawak Indians, who arrived, probably, around AD 200 in their attempt to escape from the war-loving Caribs. The Arawaks brought with them agricultural and ceramic traditions, and remains of their villages and artefacts can be seen on more than a dozen sites on the island. They were mainly fishermen and they were the people the Spanish would have met in the sixteenth century.

History is full of instances where an event that has been accepted as fact for decades suddenly becomes highly contentious. The circumstances surrounding Saint Lucia's 'discovery' are a case in point. Generations of Saint Lucians grew up believing that their island was discovered by Christopher Columbus in 1502. In recent years, however, the truth of this story has been seriously undermined. Historians now insist that Columbus never set foot on 'Fair Helen'. And whereas the islanders continue to mark the anniversary of Saint Lucia's discovery on 13 December, the great pomp and ceremony once associated with that observance have disappeared and the word is that the exact date of the island's discovery is unknown.

Information which has recently come to light suggests that another famous, though lesser-known explorer who went by the name of Juan de la Cosa could have discovered Saint Lucia in 1499 or 1504. De la Cosa was said to have sailed with Columbus on his first and second voyages. According to the historians, however, both Columbus and de la Cosa failed to mention the existence of land in the area of Saint Lucia and so the latter sailor should also surrender the honour of the island's discovery. The most likely explanation is that de la Cosa sailed past Saint Lucia and Columbus sailed, in fact, around nearby Martinique.

Exactly which Spaniard gave the island its name of Santa Lucia, after the virgin who died in Sicily in AD 304 for her Christian faith, remains unknown to this day.

The first recorded mention of the island occurs in a (Spanish) Royal Cedula – a document dividing up the New World – in 1511. De la Cosa in his map of 1500, however, shows an island named El Falcon, presumably Saint Lucia.

Around 1500, a French privateer named François de Clerc, but known to the French as Jambe de Bois, or 'Wooden Leg', is on record as having made a hideout at Pigeon Point, off the northern coast of the island, from where he harassed Spanish vessels. Half a century later, the Dutch built a fort at Vieux Fort in the south. But the first attempt at colonization was in 1605, when 67 English settlers on their way to Guiana on board the ship *Olive Blossom*, were blown off course and landed near Vieux Fort. The local Caribs sold them some huts, but five weeks later there were only nineteen survivors left and they soon fled from the island in a Carib boat.

The next attempt at colonization, in 1639, again by the British, this time under the command of Sir Thomas Warner, also failed when all the settlers were either killed or driven out by the Caribs. The French arrived in 1651 when the island was bought by two representatives of the French West India Company. Eight years later the disputes over ownership between England and France launched more than 150 years of hostilities that were to see Saint Lucia pass to and fro between the two sides up to fourteen times until being finally ceded to the British in 1814.

Soufriere became the first town to be established – by the French in 1746. Others followed rapidly, all with French names. By 1780, twelve towns were in existence. It was during this time, on 23 June

▲ Soufriere and the Pitons

Plantation House, Mamiku

1763 to be precise, that the future Empress Josephine of France was born at Paix Bouche, in the north of the island. The ruins of the estate house where she was born can still be seen.

In 1765, two Frenchmen started the sugar industry at Vieux Fort. Over the next fifteen years, nearly fifty estates were in operation or under construction. A devastating hurricane of 1780 left Saint Lucia in ruins, but the industry was quickly restored, requiring the importation of slaves from West Africa.

▲ Military ruins are reminders of Saint Lucia's turbulent past

The wars between France and Britain prevented the growth of very large plantations as on other Caribbean islands and the abolition of slavery in 1838 also meant that much of the land on the island was not used as intensively. Sugar continued to be grown until the decline of the industry in Saint Lucia in the 1960s.

The year 1782 is another memorable one in the island's history, for it was then that Admiral George Rodney, who had established his British navy in the 'second best' natural harbour in the Lesser Antilles, Gros Islet Bay, sailed to engage the French under Admiral de Grasse in the Dominica Passage. Pigeon Island (as it was then) had afforded him an observation point where he could watch the French on Martinique. The ruins of his fort are still there. The ensuing naval battle resulted in a major defeat for the French and was called the Battle of the Saints. But the hostilities were far from over. The year 1795 was one of the most bloody on the island and with the Anglo-French conflict raging in full fury most of Saint Lucia's towns and villages were destroyed. Then in the following year, when the island was repossessed by the British, Castries was burnt to the ground.

In 1796, General Moore launched an attack on the French, who were encamped on Morne Fortuné (perhaps the most fought-over part of the island), overlooking Castries. After two days of intense fighting, the 27th Inniskilling Regiment forced the French to surrender. A monument to that heroic victory stands on the former battleground today. The architecture of Fort Charlotte, which stands on the crest of the hill, bears witness in its mixed styles of stone and brick construction to the frequent changes of ownership it underwent.

In 1812, Castries was again destroyed by fire. Five years later another hurricane caused widespread destruction on the island. By 1827 England's influence had begun to assert itself in Saint Lucia when English commercial law was introduced. In 1838, after the slaves were freed, Saint Lucia was included in the Windward Islands with the seat of government in Barbados. Four years later, the English language was formally established.

However, one important legacy of the island's French cultural history is the patois or Creole dialect spoken by the overwhelming majority of the islanders, and similar to that heard in Haiti and Mauritius. A visitor is bound to hear much of this 'broken French' at every turn while on the island. Phrases like 'Bon Ju' (Good morning), 'Ki le i ye?' (What time is it?) 'Mwe vlé o bwé' (I would like a drink) and 'Es u émé najé?' (Would you like to swim?) may sound strange to the visitor, but they are all part of this extensive dialect which, although it has now become acceptable as a real means of communication, was frowned upon in certain circles up until fairly recently.

The coaling industry was started in 1863 when the first steamship called at Port Castries, which was to become a major coaling port in this part of the world for almost a century. The growth of the industry demanded labourers, and by 1882 the first shipment of indentured Indian workers arrived on the island. Many more arrived in the following thirty years; some returned but the majority chose to stay, and they provide yet another aspect to Saint Lucia's population.

Several international events affected industry in the early part of the twentieth century, among them being the abandonment of the island as a garrisoned naval station in 1906, the opening of the Panama Canal in 1914, the First World War, the world depression beginning in 1929, and finally, the introduction of oil and diesel to fuel ships in the 1940s. In 1927 and then again in 1948, the capital, Castries, was further ravaged by fire, on the latter date most of the commercial sector being destroyed.

By 1929, Saint Lucia was in touch with the outside world by air and sea-plane and was no longer wholly dependent on the sea for transport and communications beyond her shores. During the Second World War, the United States established bases on the island and military airports were built near Gros Islet and Vieux Fort.

In 1951, citizens of Saint Lucia over the age of twenty-one received the right to vote, and a new Constitution for the Windward Islands (the seat of government then being in Grenada) was enacted. Saint Lucia joined the West Indies Federation in 1958, but it collapsed in 1962. A new Constitution came into being in 1960, with the first Ministers of Government being appointed. This Constitution was to last until 1967, when Britain gave the island full self-government. In 1979, the last colonial link was severed when Saint Lucia achieved full independence.

④ Government

Saint Lucia is a constitutional monarchy and has enjoyed a parliamentary system of government for several decades. The Head of State is Great Britain's Queen Elizabeth II, represented on the island by a Governor General, who holds office at Her Majesty's pleasure, although the holder of the office is usually recommended by the Prime Minister, who heads the Government of Saint Lucia.

The Prime Minister is selected from among the members of the party that wins a majority of seats in a general election, held every five years. The Prime Minister and his Cabinet of Ministers have executive authority while legislative authority is controlled by the Parliament.

The island has a bicameral legislature with a seventeen-member House of Assembly composed of elected members, and a Senate of eleven, appointed by the Governor General (two members), the Prime

▼ Governor General's House

Minister (six members) and the Leader of the Opposition (three members). No person can sit in both chambers of Parliament.

The Constitution also provides for a Parliamentary Commissioner, or Ombudsman, and an Integrity Commission, both appointed by the Governor General acting on the advice of the Leader of the Opposition.

The judicial system consists of Magistrates' Courts, a High Court and Court of Appeal, and the Privy Council in Britain. St Lucia has signed to become a member of the Caribbean Court of Justice (CCJ) to replace the Privy Council in the region.

For more than a century and a half, Saint Lucia experienced colonial government by Britain. After the Treaty of Paris in 1763, the British government decided to adopt firmer measures in the administration of its colonies in the West Indies. Representative government was considered an obstacle to the policy of bettering the conditions for the mass of the population. In 1817, by Royal Proclamation, a Privy Council was established, comprising an executive and legislative body, to serve the colonies, but was abolished fifteen years later, and separate Legislative and Executive Councils were set up on each island. This system remained in force for nearly a century.

After the First World War, the educated classes in the West Indies began agitating against Crown Colony Government. This was no new issue, but the stirrings of social and political dissension which followed the war brought the complaints and grievances of the people to the surface. For the first time, Saint Lucians began expressing their dissatisfaction with colonial government and their desire for representative government, whereby they would elect their own people to run their affairs.

In 1924, after a visit to the region by a British government official, a form of semi-representative government was granted to the island which, however, left elected members in the minority. Nominated members appointed by the Colonial Governor dominated. The cry for full representation of the mass of the population and participation in government continued, and in 1935 a new Constitution was enforced, but full power still eluded the islanders.

The birth of the trade union movement in the 1930s took the struggle further, forcing Britain to send a one-man Commission to the island in 1938. In his report, Lord Moyne said that the claims for full representation were warranted, in order to give Saint Lucians a greater voice in the management of their own affairs. He also pointed out that the growing political consciousness on the island

▲ Museum display

was sufficiently widespread to make it doubtful that any reform, social or otherwise, would be completely successful unless accompanied by the greatest measure of constitutional development that he considered 'judicious' in the circumstances.

The Second World War, which came shortly after the Commission, further fired the ideals of democracy and independence in Saint Lucia, as it did in other parts of the region. In 1951, a major development took place, with the attainment of universal adult suffrage. Before that, only people with property could vote. Now the qualification was merely that the prospective voter should be over twenty-one years old and should live on the island. The demands of the Saint Lucians seemed to have been met. In addition, the Legislative Council was rearranged to give elected members a clear majority. But as far as the executive body was concerned, elected members were still in a position whereby the British Governor or Administrator had the power to over-ride the advice and wishes of the executive, if he so chose. In effect, the earlier frustrations remained.

The agitation continued until meaningful change came with the introduction of a ministerial system of government, and elected members dominated both the Legislative and Executive Councils. Under this system, the executive became the chief policy-making instrument. The emergence of political parties a few years earlier meant that politicians could now take full advantage of the Constitution, although the Administrator still wielded considerable authority, including control over the finances of the island. The Audit Department was independent of any ministry, and internal security, defence, labour, migration, external affairs and matters not relating to the portfolios of the ministers were kept under his control.

A Federation of the West Indies, advocated by Britain in the previous century, finally came into being in 1958, with Saint Lucia as a member. The idea was that all the former British islands and territories would come together as one independent nation. However, the experiment was short-lived and was abandoned in 1962 when Jamaica and later Trinidad – the two largest countries – withdrew. The West Indian islands began to drift apart, each proceeding to full independence on their own. Efforts to unite Barbados and the Windward and Leeward Islands, including Saint Lucia, and later the Windward and Leewards alone both failed. By the mid-1960s, Saint Lucia had joined the trek of the small West Indian islands going to Britain to negotiate their freedom from colonialism.

In 1967 the island attained self-government, and in 1979 full independence. In that same year, Saint Lucia became a member of the Commonwealth of Nations, joined the Organization of American States and became the 142nd member of the United Nations. Saint Lucia is a member of the Organization of Eastern Caribbean States and the Caribbean Community (CARICOM) and the Common Market. France, the People's Republic of China, Venezuela, Mexico and Cuba all have resident Ambassadors in Saint Lucia and there is a British High Commissioner as well. Other countries with diplomatic representation are the Dominican Republic, Guyana, Germany, Italy, Jamaica, the Netherlands, Norway, Denmark and Sweden.

⑤ A man named Bideau

In the heart of the city of Castries, a monument has been erected to a national hero whom Saint Lucians have only recently come to know. In the centre of the Square christened Place Bideau, bronze busts of the Venezuelan liberator Simon Bolivar, and a Saint Lucian, Jean Baptiste Bideau, sit a few yards apart in memory of two great men from different backgrounds whose association more than a century and a half ago was to shape the destiny of a large part of the continent of South America.

Although Saint Lucia is a country rich in history, it is mainly a history that has been dominated over the centuries by foreign figures – soldiers and adventurers from present-day metropolitan countries that were once colonial powers. In recent times, that pattern has changed somewhat as Saint Lucia's historians began to unearth the names of their own national heroes. For instance, history now records the feats of some of those local figures who fought courageously against the British forces in Saint Lucia in the eighteenth century. Recently, a French mulatto named Jean Baptiste Bideau has joined the ranks of those Saint Lucians whose heroic feats have been demanding official recognition, although it has not been too long since Bideau's exploits in the Venezuelan War of Independence in the early eighteenth century have come to light. It is the story of a man who became deeply embroiled in one of the most bitter conflicts in the hemisphere – in the cause of a country that was not his own.

Bideau was born in 1770, in the eastern Saint Lucian settlement of Desruisseaux which still exists today. In fact, scores of his descendants still live there, bearing the same surname. A sailor by profession, Bideau made his home in Trinidad where he owned a boat-making workshop. By the time he was thirty, he had already started to mix actively in Venezuelan affairs after a distinguished service as a sea captain of Victor Hughes in Guadeloupe on behalf of the French Republic.

By 1811, with the Venezuelan conflict already brewing, Bideau put his brigantine *Boton de Rosa* at the disposal of the Venezuelan patriots. Thus began a six-year involvement in a war that was to take him from his lucrative business in Trinidad to his courageous death on Venezuelan soil.

The first battles of the war brought mixed results for the patriots. In 1813, Bideau was in the famous expedition from Chacachacare and

JEAN BAPTISTE BIDEAU

c. 1770 – 1817

BORN AT DESRUISSEAUX IN SAINT LUCIA

A SEA CAPTAIN WHO
DEDICATED HIS LIFE
TO FREEDOM, AND
HEROICALLY SAVED
THE LIFE OF
SIMON BOLIVAR

Bust of Jean Baptiste Bideau

27

was later appointed Chief of the Government of Guiria from where he was forced to flee for his life in 1815. Later, Bideau arrived in Los Cayos, Haiti, where he met Bolivar. After a series of military defeats, Bideau suggested to Bolivar the details of a plan for the invasion of Venezuela and accompanied Bolivar in his attempt to land at Ocumare de la Costa. But disaster befell the patriots, for in the attack their forces were scattered. Bolivar suddenly found himself alone on a deserted beach surrounded by the enemy, and it was then that Bideau enacted the most heroic deed of his life when he managed to seize a boat and rescue Bolivar. Fourteen years later, Bolivar, in a letter to a friend, was to recall the details of that incident. He wrote:

> I had been deceived at the time by an aide-de-camp … and by the foreign seamen who had committed the most vile act in the world. They abandoned me among my enemies on a deserted beach. I was going to shoot myself when one of them, Monsieur Bideau, returned from the sea in a boat and saved me.

In April 1817, the patriots launched their final assault, at Casa Fuerte de Barcelona, and in one of the bloodiest battles of the conflict Bideau was among the thousand men killed on both sides. But his efforts were not in vain. Bolivar lived on and went on to liberate several countries in South America, including his native Venezuela.

⑥ The people of Saint Lucia

The earliest inhabitants of Saint Lucia were Amerindians from South America, but very few present-day Saint Lucians are descended from them. The overwhelming majority of Saint Lucia's population is of African extraction, descendants of former slaves.

After the abolition of slavery in 1838, indentured labourers were brought in from India and by 1971 a total of 4000 had arrived. Although their descendants can be found all over the island there are communities like Forestiere in East Castries and Augier in Laborie and L'Abbayee and Marc in South Castries where large concentrations of

▲ St Lucians

Indians can still be found. They continue to play a considerable part in Saint Lucia's affairs to this day. People of mixed race at present form about a quarter of the population in Saint Lucia.

The average age of the population of Saint Lucia is becoming younger all the time. According to the most recent census, the population in 2001 was 157 898, of whom 60 per cent were under the age of 30. There were less than 10 000 persons over the age of 70. The population is currently growing at a rate of 1.24 per cent and the average life expectancy has been increasing for both men (72.5 years) and women (75.5 years). The infant mortality rate is 13.6 per cent.

The early French influence brought Christianity to the island and about 70 per cent of the population now belong to the Roman Catholic faith. The Catholic Church is indeed a very important feature of most of the villages and towns. Other prominent denominations include the Anglican Church, the Seventh Day Adventists, the Methodist Church, the Salvation Army and a number of Baptist and Pentecostal groups. Religion has had a great influence on the life and

▼ Schoolchildren at Gros Islet

▲ Woman in national dress

▲ Local man with drum

culture of Saint Lucians. Apart from the spiritual aspect, it has provided educational and welfare resources as well as giving a sense of continuity and stability to the island community. About 60 per cent of the population live between Castries and the northern town of Gros Islet. The rest are spread around the other towns and villages. Several housing estates have sprung up over the years like Sans Soucis, Entrepot, Ravine Chabot, the Morne, Bonne Terre, Careille, Rodney Bay and Beausejour.

Although English is the official language, most Saint Lucians speak a French patois called Kweyol. For generations, Kweyol was mainly spoken by persons in the rural areas and was often shunned elsewhere, but lately Saint Lucia has been embracing what many consider its 'first language' to the extent that Kweyol dictionaries, books and radio and television programmes have become commonplace, and its use is for the first time being permitted in the island's Parliament.

⑦ Castries – past and present

Saint Lucia's capital city, Castries, is among the most modern in the Eastern Caribbean, an achievement it owes, ironically, mainly to disaster. Between 1796 and 1948, Castries was ravaged by four enormous fires, the last wiping out most of the commercial sector. Out of the ashes, however, has sprung the modern bustling city which is possibly one of the best laid-out urban areas anywhere in the region. Nevertheless, the past is still with us in Castries and indeed it is here, possibly more than anywhere else on the island, that Saint Lucia's dual Anglo-French heritage is most evident. In the heart of Castries, many old wooden French houses still stand, with their attractive latticework and balconies. They have been well cared for and greatly enhance the face of a city which, it seemed at times, was destined to die by fire.

Castries is situated in one of the most beautiful locations in the Caribbean, being built on the shores of an almost land-locked harbour, surrounded by hills. Much of Saint Lucia's history revolves around this magnificent seaport of Castries. Its strategic position at the centre of the Eastern Caribbean chain has brought shipping from many parts of the world and here also routes from all over the islands converge. Much of Castries is located at sea-level on the island's picturesque north-west coast. The approaches to the harbour are wide and deep. The entrance is guarded by the Vigie Peninsula to the north and Tapion to the south, each with a lighthouse as a warning to mariners.

The harbour of Castries is usually a hive of activity. In recent years the port has been modernized and now handles containerized cargo, so that Castries has become an important trans-shipment centre in the Eastern Caribbean. Opposite the main harbour is a magnificent yacht basin with allied services, which, in addition to the nearby George F.L. Charles Airport, make Castries well able to welcome her many visitors.

Around the year 1785, Castries was named after the Minister of the French Navy and the Colonies, Marechal de Castries, who had played a key role in retaining the French hold on Saint Lucia two years earlier. Before that, as early as 1700, the town was referred to simply as 'Le Carenage', because of its position at the far end of a creek on the right of the harbour. Carenage means a place where boats can be

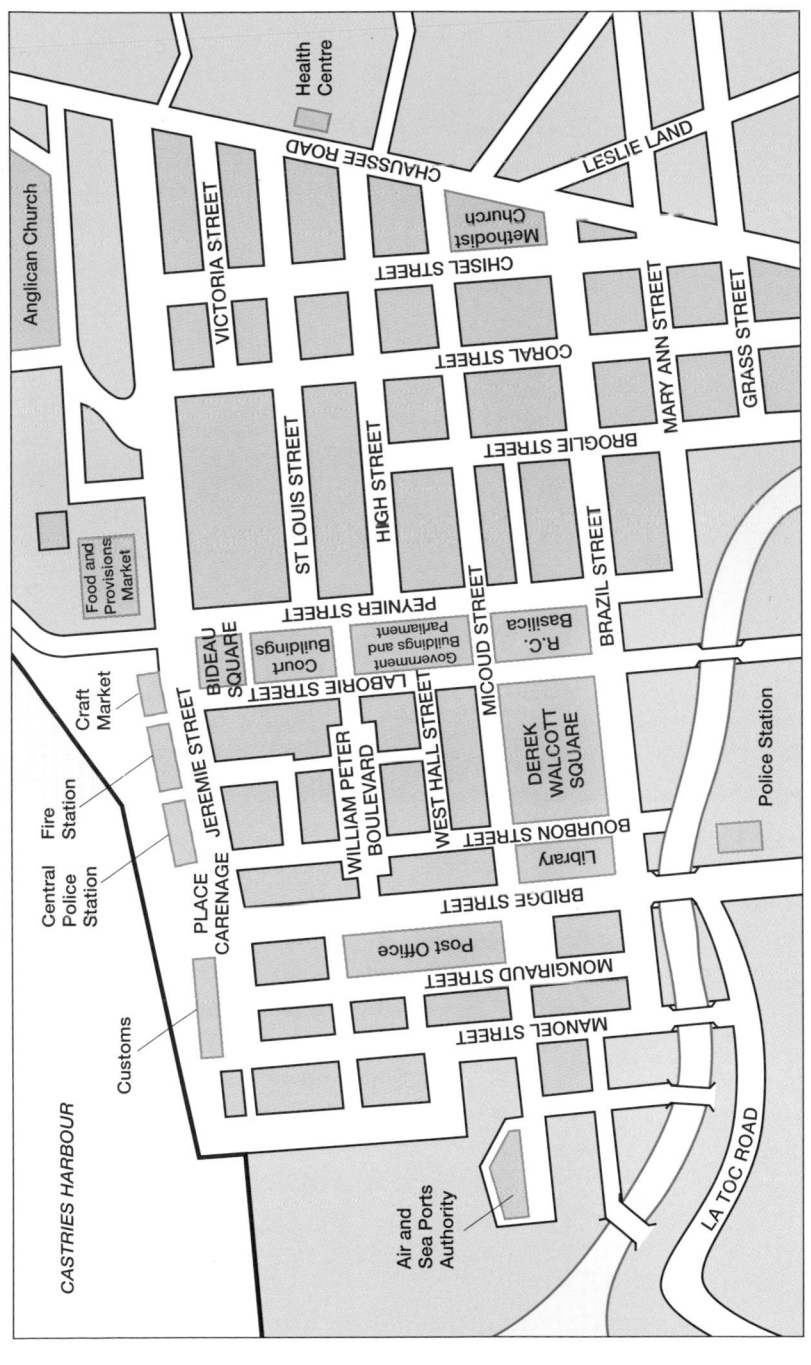

▲ Castries street plan

▲ Castries harbour from Morne Fortuné

careened. In 1746, a plan for the town was drawn up. It included a church, a place d'armées and an administrative building. But Carenage was a most unhealthy town – exposed, vulnerable and isolated – so that by 1763 plans had been drawn up to transfer it to a more suitable site at the end of the harbour. Five years later, the Castries of today began to take shape in an area beneath the fortress of Morne Fortuné where it would be more sheltered and secure. But the name 'Carenage' had a bad reputation in the West Indies, because of its unhealthy conditions; it represented fever, sickness and death, and thus frightened visitors. By 1770, the citizens were clamouring for a change of name and settled for Castries, much against the Marechal's will.

By 1850, Castries had attained such prominence that it had a Mayor with a fully elected municipality well before any of its counterpart towns in the Eastern Caribbean. However, after twenty-

one years, internal dissension led to the dissolution of that body and its replacement by a fully nominated Board. In 1967, however, Castries was elevated to 'city' status once more.

It was only just over a century ago when steam replaced sail that Castries rose to international prominence as a coaling station for the British Navy. With its natural endowment of good harbour and shipping facilities, it became the leading coaling port in the West Indies with three major international companies bunkering ships there simultaneously. At that time, thousands of rural people came to Castries to find work, and the town expanded rapidly. Prosperous merchants built large houses on the hillsides and new suburbs appeared on the edge of the old town.

With prosperity, however, came some violent incidents. In 1905 the British withdrew their troops from Saint Lucia, leaving only a small police force to maintain law and order. In 1907, coal carriers called a strike to protest about working conditions at the Castries harbour. This event triggered off uprisings in other parts of the island where

Castries market scenes

grievances over industrial relations had been brewing for some time. Rioters destroyed food shops in Castries, the main food market was looted and labourers at Cul-de-Sac joined the strike and marched on the capital. At Roseau, another band of workers attacked the police station and there was much violence. In the meantime, police reinforcements were summoned from nearby Barbados and Saint Vincent. These, together with the timely arrival of a British warship, quelled the disturbance.

After 1920, when the coal boom ended and trade declined, Castries underwent a quieter period. During the Second World War, the town was again in the international headlines when a German submarine sneaked into the harbour and torpedoed two ships berthed there. With independence, Castries became a real capital city. Because of its expanding civil service and being also at the centre of the banana-export and tourist industry, its population grew to comprise about 40 per cent of Saint Lucia's total population.

Today, few traces of the city's earlier fame are visible to the visitor, but its reputation as a major port remains. Castries has become a well-established city and is always ready to receive visitors. If you arrive by cruise ship, you alight on the city's doorstep, close to Saint Lucia's main area of commercial activity. If you come by air, arriving at George F.L. Charles Airport, you drive alongside miles of sandy beaches on the way to your hotel.

The main shopping centre contains a wide range of gift and souvenir shops, restaurants and banking facilities. The Derek Walcott Square (previously Columbus Square) to honour the Nobel Laureate, with its impressive monument to Saint Lucia's world war victims and its enormous saman tree – the largest and oldest on the island – is another popular tourist attraction.

A visit to the Castries market – especially at weekends – gives the visitor an insight into the Saint Lucian's diet with its wide variety of typical West Indian fruits and vegetables: mangoes, oranges, pawpaws, water-melons, sour-sop, bananas, carrots, dasheen, cucumbers, sweet potatoes, yams … the list goes on. Hand woven or plaited handicraft items from hats to bags and from brooms to rugs attest to the talent of the Saint Lucian people.

The physical face of Castries has undergone a dramatic change over the last quarter century. Nowhere is this transformation more evident than on the waterfront where dilapidated shacks and swamplands have been replaced by high-rise office blocks, and important business and commercial organizations like the Saint Lucia Fish Marketing

Corporation and Saint Lucia Electricity Services are located there. Residential houses are gradually being phased out from the city centre which is becoming increasingly commercialized.

A tour of this bustling little city reveals some interesting buildings like the fascinating Victorian Library, the Roman Catholic Cathedral of the Immaculate Conception, the early wooden buildings of French design nearby in Derek Walcott Square. The hills surrounding Castries, including the Vigie Peninsula on the north side of the harbour, and Morne Fortuné, have some fine examples of mellowed-brick, eighteenth-century military buildings which have been restored and which were once the sites of fierce battles between the French and the English.

▲ Castries Cathedral

⑧ Let's tour Saint Lucia

So you have arrived in Saint Lucia and have been whisked away to your hotel; or maybe you have arrived on a cruise ship and have but a few hours on the island before you continue your cruise. Either way, most likely you will feel an immediate urge to get out and explore this truly fascinating tropical paradise. 'No sweat', as they say in Saint Lucia. You may wish to hire a car or take a taxi or minibus. Several international car rental companies like Avis, Hertz and Budget Rent-a-Car operate on the island. Also there are any number of local companies like Courtesy Car Rental, St Lucia National Car Rental, Guy's Car Rental and Cost Less Rent-a-car. If you desire to drive yourself around, you must be in possession of a valid driver's licence from your home country. Additionally you will be required to purchase a temporary licence at a small fee. As in Britain, driving is on the left side of the road. Taxis are plentiful, drivers are friendly and most cabs are comfortable, even on the narrow roads outside Castries. For standard fares, there is a fixed list. For longer journeys, you may bargain if the fare seems high. Once you have decided on your transport you are ready to set off and experience for yourself the unforgettable, spectacular natural beauty of

▲ Hibiscus

▶ Bougainvillea

the island, whose landscape is also more varied and interesting than most other Caribbean islands.

We shall assume our starting point is the capital city. Ten minutes drive out of Castries finds you above the city taking in a tremendous panorama that includes most of the scenic north-west coast, including the port of Castries. Along the way you can also catch glimpses of some of the island's flora: poinsettia, bougainvillea, hibiscus, ixora, cassia, frangipani, breadfruit and more. You must pause on Morne Fortuné (Good Luck Hill) and take time to explore this vast historical spot. Here can be seen Government House, the official residence of the Governor General and one of the few remaining examples of Victorian architecture. Morne Fortuné was one of the major battlefields in the Caribbean in the eighteenth and nineteenth centuries, when Britain and France struggled for supremacy over each other. You can wander around the old barracks and take in the commanding view stretching from the north of the island to the south. Some drivers may know where the caves once used for ammunition storage are located. Today, many of the barracks and guardrooms have been tastefully refurbished and transformed

▼ Flamboyant

into an educational complex, named after Nobel Laureate the late Sir Arthur Lewis, but the visitor can still see the following relics of the British and French military presence.

Apostles' Battery

This nineteenth-century fortification undoubtedly got its name from its four gun-embrasures. This gun emplacement lies to the west of Morne Fortuné and is near to the Castries–Cul-de-Sac highway, just off the entrance to Ciceron. Its construction was started on 16 December 1888 and it was intended for the defence of Port Castries. The four 10-inch guns, which were mounted, were specifically designed for use against iron-clad ships.

Combermere Barracks

These three military buildings were erected about the middle of the nineteenth century. The buildings were allowed to fall into a state of disrepair, but have now been restored and are in use as part of the island's principal educational complex – the Sir Arthur Lewis Community College. They are believed to have been named in honour of Captain-General Lord Combermere, who was Commander of the forces stationed in the Windward and Leeward Islands from 1817 to 1820.

Guardroom, stables, cells

These buildings, not far from the entrance to the Radio Saint Lucia Studios, are thought to be among the oldest on Morne Fortuné. Dating from the late 1770s, the ruins consist of three cells, a guardroom and stables for the horses. Some of the rings for tethering the horses can still be seen in the walls.

Halfmoon Battery

This fortification was originally built by the French in 1752 and renamed in about 1797. It was at one time a gun emplacement for three 18-pounders and two 24-pounders. A shot-oven, built about 1780, was later re-sited there.

Iron Barracks

The building consists of a framework of cast iron filled with masonry and plaster. It was built between 1829 and 1833. After several decades of disuse it was restored.

Prevost's Redoubt

This gun emplacement is among the best preserved at Morne Fortuné. It was built in 1782 and now provides a wonderful view of the island's north-west coast, and even a very good view of Martinique on clear days.

Military cemetery

Here the remains of both French and British soldiers lie buried, some since the year 1782. Many of those interred were, in fact, very young. There is also an obelisk erected in honour of four governors who died in Saint Lucia between 1829 and 1834. A fifth governor also lies buried in this cemetery. For those who are interested in this period of history, those tombstones that are still legible tell interesting stories.

From Morne Fortuné, the journey is downhill into the Cul-de-Sac

▼ Marigot Bay

▲ Guide at Sulphur Springs

and Roseau valleys, the lifeline of Saint Lucia's economy. Here you will drive through miles of banana plantations. Between Cul-de-Sac and Roseau lies Marigot Bay, one of the most beautiful coves in the Caribbean.

In recent years, this area has become a popular film location: it provided the setting for some of the film scenes of *Doctor Dolittle* and *Fire Power* for instance. Further back in history, in 1778, the British Admiral Samuel Barrington sailed into Marigot harbour after being pursued by Count d'Estaing of the French fleet and managed to camouflage his ships successfully by tying large palm fronds to the masts.

From Marigot Bay, the next important stop will have to be at Soufriere, home of the towering Pitons and the Sulphur Springs. The Pitons will, no doubt, both startle and amaze you with their magnificence: two giant peaks, the Gros Piton and the Petit Piton, rising up over half a mile, seemingly side by side but in fact several miles apart and virtually from out of the sea. It is believed they were formed millions of years ago as a result of volcanic activity. Nearby are

▼ Fishing scene, Soufriere

the Sulphur Springs in the crater of what Saint Lucians call 'the world's only drive-in volcano'.

Soufriere is an attractive fishing and tourist town and full of character. Here too, is a former film location (*Water*, starring Michael Caine, was filmed here in 1984). On a visit to the nearby Anse Chastanet Hotel you may, if you are in luck, find yourself staying in one of the bungalows occupied by Christopher Reeve while filming parts of Superman II. At the Ladera Resort, not far away, Superman picked a red 'immortal' flower to take back to Lois. Ladera is on a ridge looking out over the Pitons.

To the east, on the other side of the ridge, are the Sulphur Springs and Mount Gimie (3145 feet/959 m) with its lush rainforest. Surrounding Ladera are tropical groves and small plantations. Occasional brief tropical showers provide the necessary moisture for plant growth and spring water. There are exotic tropical flowers in profusion. Ladera is part of the old Rabot plantation, which is still in operation, producing a range of crops like copra, cocoa and bananas.

By this time, if you feel in need of refreshment, what better place for a 'bite' than at one of the many Soufriere restaurants?

▼ Dennery

The road between Soufriere and Fond St Jacques then takes you up into high country for spectacular views of the surrounding mountains and valleys and right through the lush rainforest. Perhaps at this point, if you prefer a more leisurely pace, you may choose to return to your base and resume the trip another day.

The town of Vieux Fort is at the southernmost end of the island. Here the land is open and flat, quite a contrast from the earlier mountainous terrain. Vieux Fort is the location of Saint Lucia's international airport, appropriately named Hewanorra, the island's old Amerindian name. Vieux Fort is an industrial area and Saint Lucia's second most important town. Here there is a museum, which will give you more information on Saint Lucia's heritage.

At Moule à Chique, a mountain peak on the southern peninsula, you can see the turquoise Caribbean Sea merging with the blue Atlantic. Off in the distance, a mere twenty miles away, there is a glimpse of the neighbouring island of St Vincent. On the Atlantic side of Vieux Fort, the tiny Maria Islands rise from the sea. Now declared a nature reserve, the Maria Islands are inhabited by five species of amphibians and reptiles, three of which have not been found, so far, in other parts of the world, and the other two nowhere else in the Caribbean.

▲ Pigeon Point

From Vieux Fort, the journey continues along the 33-mile highway linking the southern town to Castries. On the way are the 'twin' villages of Micoud and Dennery, both important agricultural areas. Soon you come to another nature reserve called Fregate Islands, a roosting place for the fregate bird and a natural habitat for Saint Lucia's own species of the boa constrictor. As your vehicle winds its way down, you will take in the Barre de L'Isle ridge of mountains in the centre of the island and look several miles down the valley where a network of rivers carries water down through a lush covering of forest ferns and flowering plants.

The final leg of your round-the-island tour will take you northwards and to the Pigeon Island National Park. Here can be found relics of the island's earlier history, particularly those of Carib culture. A home for the earlier Amerindians and a base for pirates in the sixteenth

century, Pigeon Island came into military prominence when it was fortified by the British in 1778. It was from here that in 1782 Admiral Rodney sailed with the British fleet to defeat the French under Admiral de Grasse in the Battle of the Saints. Ruins of military installations and a former cemetery still remain. Pigeon Island once stood on its own off the coast but in recent years it has been joined to the mainland by a causeway. The area has been converted into a national park and there are a museum and a restaurant. The park is among several places of interest being 'guarded' by the Saint Lucia National Trust, a non-governmental organization established in 1984 to conserve the natural and cultural heritage of Saint Lucia for present and future generations.

If there is still time, or perhaps on another day, your guide could drive you to Paix Bouche in the north-east of the island. This was the

Reduit Beach

birthplace of Josephine Tascher de la Pagerie, future wife of Napoleon and Empress of France. She was born here in June 1763 and later christened in neighbouring Martinique. The family lived on Saint Lucia until 1771 and ruins of their estate home still remain to be seen.

Saint Lucia is endowed with beautiful beaches, several of which stretch for miles. Pigeon Point, near the town of Gros Islet, is one of these outstanding beaches, as is Jack's Beach at Cap Estate in the north, which is one of the most secluded bathing areas on the island. Reduit Bay, not far away, is recommended. Moving back closer to Castries there are the popular Choc Bay and Vigie Beach. These are all white-sand beaches, but if you prefer something different, there is the black volcanic sand beach in Soufriere.

Several hotels have planned tours for their guests. In addition there are independent tour companies offering anything from hikes to boat, helicopter and plantation tours and from whale watching to submarine tours to see the island's reefs, sunken ships and coral gardens. The plantation tours are especially enlightening, giving the visitor a taste of both the history and culture of Saint Lucia at the same time.

A tour of the twin Fregate Islands on the eastern coast between the months of May and July gives the visitor an opportunity to see the spectacular fregate bird nesting and roosting. Over the years a number of heritage sites have been created around the island and heritage tours offer visitors a really unique Saint Lucian experience.

9 The Sulphur Springs story

Of all Saint Lucia's tourist attractions, none has achieved more international fame than the boiling Sulphur Springs. The closest competitors are the majestic Pitons. The fact that both the Sulphur Springs and the Pitons are located in the same area, Soufriere, on the south-west side of the island, gives that town a certain status in national affairs.

For the visitor, the Sulphur Springs represent something of a rarity as tourist attractions go. For Saint Lucians, they once represented a

▲ Sulphur Springs sign

potential source of geothermal energy in a developing country that was badly hit by the high prices of energy supplied on the world market.

The Sulphur Springs, which also gave Soufriere its name, are part of a low-lying volcano which last erupted many thousands of years ago. Since then, it has been active all the time, but only as a solfatara, that is, instead of lava or ashes, it emits only hot vapour and gases. The crater-like basin in which the bubbling springs are found is a caldera, a collapsed volcanic formation.

At one time, in the nineteenth century, the Sulphur Springs were part of Saint Lucia's economic history when tons of sulphur were exported, but, despite the recent interest in their development as a high-capacity energy supplier, it is as a tourist attraction that the springs will remain best known. According to the experts, the springs rate alongside the Soufriere of Ozendaki of Japan and the famous solfatara of Pozzuoli in Italy.

During the Anglo-French conflict for possession of Saint Lucia, the Sulphur Springs came into their own when Louis XVI, hearing of their medicinal qualities, ordered the building of extensive baths in the area to serve his tired troops. The steaming sulphurous water coming from the springs was pronounced beneficial for various illnesses like rheumatism, ulcers and respiratory complaints. In 1940, a French vulcanologist described the Sulphur Springs as 'the most interesting, perhaps the most potentially active, possibly the most highly curative and certainly the most accessible', of all solfatara in the world. Today, while the French troops are no longer here to use its waters, Diamond Baths, which complement the Sulphur Springs, offer the visitor the same naturally heated mineral baths that provide a unique and relaxing experience.

In the 1970s, the government of the island started exploratory work at the Sulphur Springs to check their potential as an energy source. These investigations confirmed the presence of steam, but because of the enormous outlay of funding required to bring the project on stream, it had to be abandoned. But the Sulphur Springs continue to boil, drawing visitors from all over the globe. A tour of this fascinating site is a 'must' for every visitor.

⑩ Flora and fauna

As on most tropical islands, Saint Lucia's plant and animal life is one of richness and constant discovery. In fact, Saint Lucians are, by and large, still very much uninformed about many of the exotic plants and animals that are to be found throughout the island. This results partly from an attitude of indifference which local peoples often naturally adopt in such matters. But there are many individuals and organizations on the island working steadfastly for the preservation and protection of plants and animals, some of them, especially in the latter case, unique to Saint Lucia.

If you are a visitor, however, you simply cannot be indifferent to Saint Lucia's rich flora and fauna, which are an integral part of the island's natural heritage. Several species of fauna are now extinct and efforts are under way to protect others which appear destined to suffer the same fate. One of these species is the island's national bird, the Saint Lucia parrot (*Amazona versicolor*), with its green body, blue head, red breast and yellow tail. It is unique to this area and one of the world's rarest birds. The parrot makes its home in the rainforest of the interior, where the vegetation is thick and tropical. In the past, this species of bird was so severely depleted by hunting and illegal trafficking that attempts had to be made to save it from extinction by breeding it in captivity overseas. Today, the parrot population is on the increase again. A

▲ St Lucia parrot
(Amazona versicolor)

▲ Iguana

new Wildlife Ordinance gives legal protection to the parrot and makes it illegal to hunt or traffic in this particular species.

There are many other winged creatures on Saint Lucia, but, like the parrot, their numbers are decreasing rapidly. Amongst these are doves and hummingbirds, kingbirds, warblers, herons, fregate birds and gulls. Saint Lucia has always had a rich bird population, however, in contrast to its small reptile population. The Fregate Islands and the nearby mainland provide a natural habitat for a variety of wildlife. If you are lucky, you may sight the harmless boa constrictor. The islands are under the management of the Saint Lucia National Trust which provides guides for tourists.

The iguana, a dull-grey lizard that changes its colour to blend with its surroundings, is also fading fast from the Saint Lucian scene. Some can still be found at Grande Anse, in the north-east of the island. There are also three species of tree lizards, one of them indigenous, two species of ground lizards and four of snakes, including the fer de lance and boa constrictor. On the Maria Islands, off the coast near the town of Vieux Fort, can be found the Saint Lucia whiptail, a colourful ground lizard that, ironically, bears all the four colours of the island's flag: blue, yellow, white and black. There too can be found the Saint

Tropical rainforest on Gros Piton Trail ▶

▲ Mamiku Gardens

Lucia racer, a truly rare species of grass snake. Both remain unique to the islands.

Grande Anse is important to wildlife enthusiasts. It is the nesting grounds of the leatherback turtle, acclaimed as the world's largest reptile today. Every year between March and July, these huge creatures come to Grande Anse to lay their eggs. Hawksbill and green turtles also nest on the island.

One of the early names given to Saint Lucia by the Amerindians is 'Hewanorra' which means 'where the iguana is found'. There are a few of the reptiles on the island at Louvet and Grande Anse. The huge lizards have over the years been targeted by both man and beast, including dogs and mongooses. The Forestry Department's Mini Zoo at Union is home to many examples of Saint Lucian wildlife, including the iguana.

The agouti, a rabbit-like animal, is yet another species of fauna whose days appear to be numbered. The only other indigenous mammal reported on the island, a muskrat, is now extinct.

Saint Lucia's flora is also under threat, but there are still more than 1200 species of beautiful flowering plants, shrubs and trees to be seen: hibiscus, flamboyant, frangipani, daffodil, poinsettia and a variety of lilies, including anthurium, head the list. Fruit trees are plentiful. Large banana plantations are located in the valleys and a wide variety of agricultural plants can be found everywhere. Watch out for many of Saint Lucia's exotic fruits and vegetables during your round-the-island drive: mango, avocado, lemon, orange, breadfruit, sour-sop, pawpaw, passion fruit, golden apple and sugar apple, among others.

Saint Lucia's rainforest covers some 19000 acres of lush valleys and peaks that are ideal for bird watching or just plain relaxing.

Mamiku in the village of Micoud on the east coast and Diamond Estate at Soufriere are the homes of two of the island's spectacular botanical gardens, where you will find perfect examples of local exotic vegetation. Both are family plantations with histories that are as colourful as that of the island itself.

⑪ Food, drink and shelter

The range of Saint Lucia's hospitality amenities is constantly being upgraded to fit the bill of a serious tourist resort. Where once the emphasis was on luxury hotels, some operated by the big international chains, today it is the smaller to medium-size units that are mushrooming. Not that big hotels are a thing of the past. Hardly! It is simply that the island's tourist industry has expanded so dramatically that ownership and participation in the hotel sector is now more diversified than ever before and Saint Lucians themselves are claiming a larger share of the pie.

Additionally, the large hotels (old as well as new) are revolutionizing the whole style of their operations from the 'traditional' to the new 'all inclusive' arrangement where the visitor pays just one price for his/her entire holiday (accommodation, food, drinks, recreation, taxes and service charges, and so on) even before he or she arrives on the island.

Most of the international chains of earlier years have disappeared from Saint Lucia: Holiday Inn, Halcyon, Steigenberger, Cunard, Hyatt and Club Med. There's only one big international name today, that of the Jamaican group, Sandals, which has taken over the Cunard Trafalgar's La Toc Hotel, the Halcyon Beach Hotel and more recently the Hyatt Regency, for conversion into 'all-inclusive' operations.

▲ Sandals Hotel

Several new hotels, including some quite classy ones, have gone into operation, including the Royal Saint Lucian and Windjammer Landing Villa Beach Resort on the north-western coast, and the exquisite up-market Jalousie Hilton Plantation Resort, tucked away between Soufriere's Pitons. But, for possibly the first time, small hotels (ten rooms or less) and guest houses, most of them owned by nationals, are on the increase.

The Saint Lucia Hotel and Tourism Association, which casts a keen eye over standards and service in the hotel industry, reports that total accommodation in the hotel sector is now well in excess of the 3500-room mark and increasing all the time.

Most of the hotels are located on or close to one or more of Saint Lucia's beautiful white-sand beaches and within minutes of one of the island's two commercial airports. The following is a guide to some of Saint Lucia's hotels.

Le Sport

Located at Cap Estate on the northernmost tip of the island, this hotel offers what it calls the 'body holiday', a physical fitness and beauty programme combined with the normal beach vacation, under the 'all-inclusive' arrangement. The facility comprises 150 rooms and two suites. On offer is a structured programme of body and beauty treatments, some using the beneficial mineral properties of seawater and seaweed. Sauna baths, invigorating shower massages, reflexology foot massages, land and water sports, a modern air-conditioned gym offering weight training, aerobics and even yoga are all part of the 'body holiday' package. There is also the food inspired by Michel Guérard, the French chef who made *cuisine légère* an art form. You will savour meals that are light, nutritious and flavourful, all prepared with the finest fresh ingredients.

Club Saint Lucia

The largest single hotel complex on the island, this comprises 372 rooms and caters for singles, couples, families and honeymooners all under the 'all-inclusive' concept. Spacious accommodation in single-storey units is scattered down a gently sloping hillside surrounded by extensive gardens. Here you eat and drink all you can. There is a large freshwater swimming pool and water and land sports, with instruction. Club Saint Lucia is the home of the Saint Lucia Racquet Club with seven competition-standard tennis courts, a gymnasium and squash courts. This is an ideal resort for couples planning to tie the knot. Club Saint Lucia handles several hundred weddings for visitors every year.

Royal Saint Lucian

Located a short distance away on the magnificent Reduit Beach, this is a sister hotel to the Rex Saint Lucian. The Royal, however, is a five-star hotel. Its 96 luxury suites all offer a view of the sea. The visitor arriving at the hotel's vaulted atrium entrance hall will be personally welcomed and escorted to his/her room, evidence of the experience in hotel living that the Royal offers. 'La Mirage', a large swimming pool with its own island waterfalls, a shallow pool for sunbathing and swim-up bar, the cocktail lounge, 'Le Mistral', where there is usually piano or jazz music, and the beach-side 'L'Epicure' gourmet restaurant are among the Royal's offerings. Guests can enjoy the facilities at the nearby Rex Saint Lucian Hotel.

Rex Saint Lucian

Formerly the Holiday Inn, this is a long-established favourite among Caribbean hotels. All 120 guest rooms enjoy views across the manicured lawns to the glistening Caribbean Sea. The uncrowded beach provides the perfect location for sunbathing under swaying palms, as well as for water sports or for enjoying one of the many tropical concoctions of the hotel's 'Sunset Bar'. The 'Hummingbird Bar and Restaurant' provide the venue for evening dining while the 'Flamingo' restaurant offers a romantic and elegant setting for those 'special' evenings.

Coco Kreole

Once known as Candyo Inn on Rodney Bay, it is one of the latest additions to Saint Lucia's growing list of small hotels. It comprises 20 rooms as self-catering apartments in the style of the traditional West Indian home.

Windjammer Landing Villa Beach Resort

This is a spectacular complex of Moorish-style villas built into a hillside, six miles from Castries. Altogether there are 242 suites, all luxuriously furnished. Designed to harmonize with the hillside, each villa is unique and features covered terraces and sundecks. Windjammer's two and three-bedroom villas with plunge pools offer complete privacy and relaxation, while the one-bedroom units, set amid an oasis of tropical vegetation and pools, offer the perfect setting for romance.

Bay Gardens Hotel and Bay Gardens Inn

These 'twin' hotels are also new additions to Saint Lucia's hotel stock. Bay Gardens Hotel comprises 71 rooms located along the main

▲ Windjammer Landing

Castries to Gros Islet highway at Rodney Bay. This hotel has already won several awards for service and is popular with business travellers. Its facilities include three conference rooms and a business centre. Bay Gardens Inn, which is just next door, has its own character. This is the one to go to for privacy and relaxation. It comprises 32 rooms.

Cara Suites
Located on a hillside overlooking the city, this is a favourite of corporate travellers and for conferences. It comprises 54 rooms and a complementary business centre with internet access. Another of its attractions is the elegant Mandolin Restaurant with some breathtaking views of Castries and the Caribbean Sea.

Green Parrot Inn
Popular with North Americans, this hotel on historic Morne Fortuné offers a different view of Castries and the Caribbean Sea. There are 55 rooms, each well furnished and equipped with showers, air-conditioning and balconies or patios.

Morne Fortuné Apartments
This historic building on the top of Morne Fortuné offers 12 individually decorated self-catering apartments with verandahs that provide one of the most breathtaking views of coastline and sea that

Saint Lucia can offer. A lovely swimming pool, set in the tropical gardens, overlooks the coastline and beaches below.

Saint James Club (formerly Wyndham Morgan Bay Resort)
With an eight-building complex comprising 240 rooms, this is another an 'all-inclusive' operation just half a mile from Castries and minutes away from Vigie Airport. Nestled into 22 acres of lush tropical landscape, Saint James is like no other place in the Caribbean. Coconut trees abound, and native flowers blaze with colour. There is an extensive range of recreation and leisure activities including a varied programme of entertainment that even allows guests to display their own talents.

Rendezvous, formerly Couples
Located on Vigie Beach, this is also 'all-inclusive', specializing in honeymoon packages and wedding arrangements. Its 100 rooms are surrounded by exotic flora and have sea and garden views.

Sandals
This Jamaican hotel chain has taken over the 100-acre Cunard Hotel La Toc and La Toc Suites, the beach resort located just two miles from Castries. It is now known as Sandals St Lucia Golf Resort and Spa and comprises 327 rooms. A few miles away is the Sandals Halcyon, formerly Halcyon Beach Club, which comprises another 170 rooms. Then at the northern tip of the island is Sandals Grande, the former Hyatt Regency, which comprises 284 rooms. The Sandals name is gaining great fame for its value for money and the high quality of service it gives to each guest.

Harmony Marina Suites
A small, family-operated inn of 22 one-bedroom suites and eight VIP honeymoon suites located right on the lovely Rodney Bay lagoon, the local Mecca for yachtsmen. All suites are of four- and five-star standard. Harmony's cuisine is one with a difference, excelling in Chinese, Malaysian and Indian dishes.

Auberge Seraphine
A quaint 28-room hotel located just across from George F.L.Charles Airport at Vigie Cove near Castries harbour. It is very popular with corporate visitors.

Seaview Apartel
A small family owned and operated hotel, Seaview offers personalized service. It consists of ten one-bedroom suites, seven of

which are self-contained. It is located close to a major supermarket, car rental agency and a bank.

Jalousie

Hilton Plantation Resort. Nestled in a natural garden of wondrously colourful vegetation, set against the aquamarine waters of the Caribbean, this resort, as the brochures promoting it testify, is the closest thing to paradise on earth. Indeed, Jalousie is located in an area of ground 'sacred' to most Saint Lucians: 320 acres right between the famous Pitons in Soufriere. Jalousie features 115 cottages, including 12 suites, and is operated along the 'all-inclusive' line. With a private, gently sloping beach, Jalousie has an ambience of serenity. Guests stay in private cottages along the lush green hillside flushed with red, orange and violet bougainvillea. The colourful flora is accentuated by perfectly manicured coconut palm trees swaying gently in the Caribbean breeze. Apart from the Pitons, many other natural wonders surround Jalousie.

Ladera Resort

This is also located in Soufriere. Sitting on a hillside overlooking the spectacular Pitons, it consists of seven three-bedroom villas with private pool or garden and nine suites each with an 'open wall' exposing breathtaking views of the Caribbean. Tropical flowers and trees grow in profusion. With Ladera is the newly renovated Dasheene Restaurant, which combines the best of Caribbean and Continental cuisine.

Anse Chastanet Hotel

Built on 400 acres at Soufriere, this is a secluded, romantic beach resort. It consists of 48 hillside gazebos with louvred windows, ceiling fans and private bath and balcony. There is a five-star scuba facility at Anse Chastanet which also caters for windsurfers and snorkellers, and offers a complimentary hiking programme for nature lovers.

Marigot Bay Resort

Just south of Castries lies a tranquil lagoon surrounded by lush green hills and divided by a palm-fringed finger of sand. This is Marigot Bay, the celebrated hiding place of the British fleet during the colonial wars. Author James Michener called Marigot 'the most beautiful bay in the Caribbean'. This is the setting for Marigot Bay Resort which comprises 14 waterfront cottages, 10 one- and two-bedroom hillside villas and eight double lanai studios. An incredible choice of sea and land activities is available. Two fine restaurants grace the resort including 'Dolittle's Restaurant and Bar' named after the movie Doctor Dolittle, which was filmed on Marigot Bay in the 1960s.

The Skyway Inn
The 32-room hotel is just next door to Hewanorra International Airport. Its rooms and one self-contained suite offer a perfect hideaway from hectic daily routines.

Rainbow Hotel
Providing the perfect getaway, this hotel is made up of 76 rooms in a uniquely relaxing environment and tucked away on a popular beach in the north.

Kimatrai Hotel
Located on a little hill outside the town of Vieux Fort and five minutes by car from Hewanorra International Airport, this quiet pleasant family-operated hotel contains 14 double rooms plus apartments and is suitable for families and the budget-minded visitor.

In addition, a number of fine restaurants can be found on Saint Lucia catering for both tourists and local people alike. Here is a short guide to those that offer good cuisine. Rodney Bay, however, is the mecca of fine and exotic foods offering a range of choices to suit every palate.

▲ Anse Chastenet Hotel

Bon Appétit
Situated in a cache on Morne Fortuné, this inn offers a panoramic view of Castries. Featured on the menu is authentic West Indian cooking and also a variety of American dishes cooked to order.

Chung's and Sea Town
Both located in Castries, these restaurants specialize in Chinese cuisine.

The Green Parrot Restaurant
Situated on Morne Fortuné, this restaurant is open daily for lunch and dinner and places strong emphasis on local foods and vegetables. The proprietor here, known to all as Chef Harry, is an extremely popular national figure and rated one of the island's best chefs. Chef Harry was trained at Claridge's in London and started the Green Parrot more than two decades ago. His culinary skills have earned him numerous international awards. At the Green Parrot, there is local entertainment every Monday, Wednesday and Saturday evening. On Saturday there is a floor show hosted by the Chef himself, who also sings.

Scuttlebutts
Located in the Rodney Bay Marina, Scuttlebutts' popularity is mainly among visiting yachtsmen. Good service, friendly atmosphere and waterside ambience are among its hallmarks.

The Great House
Located at Cap Estate, this restaurant takes you back in time to the days of Great House dining. Here you will find an ever-changing menu, but the emphasis is on French and West Indian cuisine. This is the place for romantic candlelit dinners in a warm atmosphere where the service, food, wines and ambience are at their very best.

La Flambé
This specializes in dishes prepared at the tableside. Located at Rodney Bay, La Flambé is superbly decorated. The food is excellent and some really great cocktails can be tried.

Restaurant Row
Located in the Gablewoods Mall, these restaurants offer a variety of servings, including Creole and American lunches and dinner, Far Eastern specialities, Mexican fast foods and home-made ice-cream.

The Bistro
Look for this at Rodney Bay. It specializes in seafood and is next door to the marina. The Bistro serves Continental and English pub fare.

The Lime
Also located at Rodney Bay. Grills and snacks, mouth-watering foods and really exotic beverages are on offer. It is within walking distance of several of the north's hotels. A favourite of locals and visitors alike. Great atmosphere especially on weekends.

Ginger Lily
At Rodney Bay, too, this restaurant serves Cantonese cuisine with a reasonably priced menu.

Burger Plus
Great fast foods, chicken, fish or burgers from two city centre outlets.

Kimlan's
Located opposite Derek Walcott Square, this is a popular meeting place. A variety of dishes and home-made ice-creams are served.

The Blue Lagoon
Situated at Gros Islet with good views of the marina, this restaurant offers a selection of seafood and Creole cooking prepared to order.

Place Creole
At Rodney Bay. Another waterside restaurant that specializes in Creole dishes.

Capone's
This is a new Italian restaurant at Rodney Bay which offers a range of prices and atmospheres. It has a variety of cuisine, from pizza to ice-cream to more formal Italian dishes.

Dolittle's
The owners of this superbly situated waterfront complex at the mouth of the famous Marigot Bay have created a setting as quaint as the name Dolittle's. Fourteen old-fashioned Caribbean cottages climb a hill above a 'gingerbread' dining room, bar and boutique. Young, enthusiastic staff provide excellent food and service to the guests who sail into Dolittle's free docking facilities or arrive by miniature ferryboat from across the bay. Here you are on the site where Twentieth-Century Fox filmed many sequences of the film *Doctor Dolittle*, starring Rex Harrison.

The Still
Formerly a rum distillery at Soufriere, this is now a good restaurant with bar and boutique. The Still is family-owned and operated. Much of the food comes from the adjoining plantation.

La Creole
There is an informal atmosphere at this Soufriere restaurant which offers a variety of Creole dishes and prides itself on its good service.

The Hummingbird
Also at Soufriere, this restaurant specializes in gourmet food. It is also has a lovely Piton view and swimming pool.

Oceana
Located at La Toc, the speciality here is seafood served in an ambience that reflects the island's rich British and French colonial era. There's a panoramic view over Castries to go along with it. The restaurant is highly rated for its excellent service.

Froggie Jacques
Once known as Jimmie's, ownership has changed over the years. Run by a French chef, it provides tranquil waterside dining in a tropical garden inside Vigie Cove.

▼ Froggie Jacques

Big Chef Steakhouse

Another of the top line restaurants in Rodney Bay. Big juicy succulent steaks are seasoned with special spices and served with sauces created by the Big Chef himself. Here, there's a challenge: consumption of a 32-ounce rib or strip steak earns the customer a certificate and the rank of 'Big Steak Master'.

Charthouse

Another of the Rodney Bay restaurants, Charthouse has firmly established a reputation for the finest and freshest seafood and the best prime US broiled steak in the world.

The Coalpot

Another of Saint Lucia's finest, this restaurant is located on the water's edge at Vigie Cove, across from the airport. Going now for well over four decades, it is truly a Saint Lucian icon providing one of the widest varieties in culinary servings available anywhere on the island.

Memories of Hong Kong

Another Rodney Bay establishment that specializes in Cantonese and Chinese cooking.

Tilly's 2X4

One of the finest Creole restaurants on the island, it is located off the Gros Islet Highway at Rodney Bay.

Café Claude

Situated at Rodney Bay, this is a restaurant for all tastes, combining Asian, French, Italian and Creole influences.

Domino's Pizza

This restaurant, located in Rodney Bay, serves really great pizzas and side dishes.

La Sikwi

The tiny west coast village of Anse la Raye's contribution to the island's extensive line of restaurants. Situated on a former sugar estate, it features a live band playing indigenous musical instruments.

Dutch Door

Located in Gros Islet town, Dutch Door specializes in seafood and local dishes. There is also the famous Dutch Door Omelette.

Dasheene

Nowhere else can you dine in the presence of the island's most famous landmarks, the Pitons. This restaurant has won many awards for its great dishes and fine wines.

La Classe

In the heart of Castries, La Classe is a pleasant town restaurant specializing in French Creole cuisine.

Golden Apple

A full and varied Caribbean experience awaits you here in Gros Islet town. Sample the best Caribbean lobster south of Jamaica; seafood and steaks are the specialities. Barbecued lambie or chicken eaten in a courtyard under a golden apple tree is a pleasant experience.

Believe it or not, we have only scratched the surface of the full range of restaurants and eating establishments that Saint Lucia offers. The possibilities are endless, to use a well-known cliché.

Most hotels and restaurants offer a wide variety of food including local food. Visitors should make a point of asking for local foods if they are not advertised. Saint Lucia has an abundance of fruit and vegetables, usually served fresh from the farms. There is the unofficial national dish of green figs and cod fish, which

▲ National dish - cod & figs (bananas)

you may not find on many hotel menus, but which will be served if requested. Our 'figs' are, in fact, bananas, Saint Lucia's prime agricultural export crop, grown all over the island.

In this lush tropical paradise, food is all around you, in the water and on the land. You can scoop it out of the sea or pick it off the trees. Because the island's history is rich in the cultures of two countries, the cooking also reflects it: the best of French, English, Creole, and of course Saint Lucian, cuisine. Saint Lucians can tempt you with baked lobster, stuffed breadfruit, and mangoes with ice-cream, delight you with banana bread, or fried plantain or breadfruit, and surprise you with pumpkin soup and boiled cucumber.

As for drinks, ask any Saint Lucian and he will surely tell you a hundred ways to make a good rum punch, the drink that really takes some beating. When you have tried one, you will realize you have never tasted anything quite like that before! Saint Lucian barmen are innovators and connoisseurs of the finest in food and drink, of course using ingredients that are distinctly local. Many have won international awards for their concoctions. And so, as with your food, there's never a dull moment with your drinks either. Do try the magnificent 'potions' that can be blended from local fruits with a

▲ Spiced rum

dash of the right liqueur. Many hotels have their 'special' – a top secret among the staff, usually. Ask for it wherever you may be staying and be prepared for a surprise that says a lot about the unique talents of the Saint Lucian people, talents that go even as far as mixing drinks! The island has its own line of alcoholic beverages, thanks to Saint Lucia Distillers Limited in Roseau which has already won a number of international awards. Be sure to ask for Bounty Rum when ordering, it's better known as 'The Spirit of Saint Lucia'. For beer lovers, don't miss out on 'Piton', a product of Windward and Leeward Brewery in Vieux Fort.

⑫ Sports and leisure

Sport represents an integral part of the Saint Lucian way of life; it is a facility that is provided for visitors as well. From lawn tennis and golf to water sports like windsurfing and scuba diving, Saint Lucian hotels have gone out of their way to cater for the enjoyment of visitors.

More than twenty tennis courts are available for public use, most of them at the bigger hotels and generally reserved for guests. Many hotels have tennis professionals available throughout the year, while others provide this service at specific times during the year.

There are golf courses at Sandals St Lucia and Cap Estate, close to northern hotels like Club Saint Lucia and Le Sport. The Cap 18-hole course is under the control of the Saint Lucia Golf and Country Club. It has a 350-yard driving range, clubhouse and bar. Squash and horse riding are also available at Cap Estate.

Cap Estate golf course

Cricket and soccer are traditional sports. The island now has one of the finest cricket venues in the Caribbean, the Beausejour Cricket Ground in Gros Islet town which has already hosted both Test and One Day International matches. Sadly, however, Saint Lucia remains the only major Eastern Caribbean island still to produce a Test cricketer.

There are several privately run gyms like Sportivo at Rodney Heights, Laborde's at La Toc and Body Inc. at the Gablewoods Mall which was started by internationally famous Rick Wayne, a Saint Lucian who won a series of titles while a competitive body-builder, including 'Mr Universe', 'Mr World' and 'Mr Britain', and for years edited such magazines as *Muscle* and *Fitness* and *Flex*.

For those visitors favouring the sea, of course, the range of sport and other attractions is also very wide. Diving facilities are available on the island. They offer beginners' lessons, group or individual dives and day-fishing trips as well. Among the species to be caught in local waters are barracuda, mackerel, kingfish, tuna, swordfish, wahoo and sailfish. Most beach hotels offer a selection of windsurfers, sunfish and other smaller sailing craft for free use or rental to guests. Larger sailing vessels, up to 60 feet in length, are available for charter from companies located at Rodney Bay and Marigot Bay, as well as at other locations on the island. Para-sailing is an exciting addition to the water sports.

▲ Beausejour Cricket Ground

▲ Body Inc. fitness trainer

Whale, bird and turtle watching have been growing in popularity, adding variety to the range of tourism-related enterprises on the island. More than two dozen species of great whales can be sighted during the year. There is a Whale and Dolphin Association which arranges tours for visitors.

If you prefer something a little more unusual, like a cruise on a tall ship, for example, this too is available, through Sunlink Tours. The 140-foot *Brig Unicorn* is one of only two fully square-rigged vessels existing in the world today. It took part in the 1976 Bicentennial Tall Ships Race and it is also famous for having been used in the widely acclaimed television serial, *Roots*. It offers a day's cruise from the Vigie Marina to the Pitons and Sulphur Springs, providing visitors with lunch and steel-band entertainment. Sunlink also organizes a range of land tours, 'safaris' and sea tours that have become quite popular with visitors. Several yacht charters operate from Marigot and Rodney Bays, and deep-sea fishing is available.

There are several other companies offering a variety of tours. One increasingly popular tour is that to the Diamond Botanical Gardens in Soufriere which takes in the gardens, waterfall, nature trail and estate, private mineral baths and lunch. Saint Lucia Representative Service operates a sightseeing trip that is highly recommended. You are collected from your hotel and taken to the brigantine, *Buccaneer*, a 100-foot, square-rigged sailing ship that takes you down the blue Caribbean Sea on the west coast to Soufriere with a sightseeing trip all arranged, followed by lunch and a further cruise to Anse Cochon Beach for swimming, and so on.

For the less adventurous, there are many safe and beautiful hiking trails on the island, including conducted tours of the lush rainforest where you may catch a glimpse of the Saint Lucia parrot, the national bird. Most operators offer guided tours of the island and whether your choice is walking, land games or water sports, your hotel will probably make all the necessary arrangements. Simply check at the front desk and ask for details.

13 Rodney Bay

One of the man-made wonders of Saint Lucia must surely be Rodney Bay, a sprawling development that has become almost a new city with a marina, some of the island's finest hotels and restaurants, its only public cinema, modern shopping malls and supermarkets and residential housing.

Before the 1970s, the Rodney Bay area was largely swamplands and good for nothing. The decision to transform it opened up real development possibilities for the island and today it is regarded as Saint Lucia's leading leisure community. Its marina is among the most complete yachting facilities in the English-speaking Caribbean. It is

Rodney Bay Marina

located in the shelter of the Rodney Bay lagoon and is currently enjoying a high international profile as the termination point for the annual Atlantic Rally for Cruisers, a gruelling 2600-mile event that originates every November from Las Palmas in the Canary Islands.

Rodney Bay is named after the British Admiral George Rodney who sailed from nearby Pigeon Island to engage and defeat the French in 1782. The bay is more than a mile in length and includes a man-made causeway linking the mainland with Pigeon Island where there are still historic military ruins that have been preserved.

Rodney Bay Marina provides a tranquil and protected enclave for up to 232 side tide berths with between 32 and 36 feet between side tides and has an overall draft of 14 feet. Each berth is supplied with its own individual meters for both water and electricity. Hot and cold showers, and toilets, are available for all berthing guests and all modern communications services are available.

The Rodney Bay boatyard provides storage for up to 100 boats, and facilities are available for repairs in wood, fibreglass, aluminum, stainless steel and bronze. Diesel engine repairs, wet and dry sandblasting, osmosis treatment and spray painting can be arranged, and there is duty-free fuel for outgoing boats.

One of the most recent additions to the facilities at the marina is a modern chandlery. Operated by the internationally acclaimed Island Waterworld, this US$150 000 business is adequately equipped to service all the needs of yachtsmen, including refitting.

Contributing to the total completeness of Rodney Bay are the several shore facilities that the marina offers. There is a shopping complex on the premises with a variety of boutiques and stores including a bakery, café, liquor store, supermarket, pharmacy, book and gift shop, car rental, travel agency, bank with ATM, restaurant and bar with swimming pool.

Rodney Bay is located just off the main northern highway into the capital city of Castries, a 15-minute drive. It sits at the heart of the island's main tourist sector with a number of fine hotels and a beautiful hillside housing development in the immediate vicinity.

14 Entertainment and shopping

Saint Lucia's tourist industry is still comparatively young and has therefore not yet developed to the extent of some of its competitors in the Caribbean. As a result, certain of the more popular forms of entertainment for tourists will not be found here. For instance, there are no casinos and the night-life – although improving all the time – is perhaps less extravagant and varied than in more established tourist areas. Still, Saint Lucia generally satisfies most of the entertainment demands of the visitors to its shores.

If you are in Saint Lucia at Carnival time you will have the opportunity to sample local calypso music at its best. Several tents operate in the weeks leading up to Carnival Monday and Tuesday and the highlight is the Calypso Monarch competition where the best go up against the reigning King. Saint Lucian calypso is providing more thrills and excitement than Carnival itself with such colourful performers as De Invader, Pep and Pelay, who has won the title six times, the last occasion singing from a wheelchair, the result of a crippling motor accident in the United States. Come Carnival Monday, hundreds of beautifully costumed revellers take to the streets, jumping and singing to the most popular calypsos of the year. Although Saint Lucia's Carnival is a long way off parity with that of Rio or even Trinidad and Tobago, it is sheer colour and excitement, an opportunity not to be missed.

▲ Carnival

▲ Calypsonian the Mighty Pelay

Lately, Saint Lucia has found a new medium with which to woo visitors: jazz. An international festival is now held annually, featuring some of the best known exponents of the art form. Herbie Hancock, Wynton, Delfeayo and Ellis Marsalis, Grover Washington Jr, Nancy Wilson, Earl Klugh, Ramsey Lewis, Will Downing, Rachel Farrell, Betty Carter, Chic Corea, Al Jarreau and George Benson are some of the big names that have appeared at the shows since 1992. The highlight is usually the final evening, a Sunday, at historic Pigeon Island, where thousands of visitors take their seats on the grass to listen to the headline performer. During Saint Lucia Jazz shows are held all over the country, the number of venues increasing year after year.

More and more islanders have been achieving international recognition for their musical skills. Among them are Luther Francois,

ENTERTAINMENT AND SHOPPING

▼ Ronald 'Boo' Hickson

▲ Saint Lucia Jazz Festival

whose genre is mainly jazz, and Ronald 'Boo' Hinkson, who led the legendary dance band, The Tru Tones, in the 1960s and has broadened his musical interests to achieve acclaim as a jazz artist as well. Both are also prolific music and song writers and have appeared all over the world playing alongside some of the 'big guns' in musical entertainment. There are compact discs available of local music, whether calypso, reggae, folk or jazz. If ever you're on the island and there's a concert featuring the Royal Saint Lucia Police Band, be sure to attend. They usually serve up a special treat.

Most of the hotels offer nightly entertainment: steel band and folk music for dancing, limbo, fire-eating, acrobatics, bottle dancing and so on, as cabaret.

In many hotels, visitors can sample real Saint Lucian folk music featuring local instruments or sway to the rhythms of the calypso. Many hotels and restaurants have 'happy hours' – when all drinks are at half price, or you get two for every one ordered for a stipulated period – or hotel manager's parties which are proving increasingly popular. Here, the visitor can meet and mingle with Saint Lucians from all walks of life.

The same sort of hospitality and carefree atmosphere pervades the northern town of Gros Islet on Friday evenings. A stone's throw from one of the main tourist zones, Gros Islet comes alive with an open-air street fair that affords a rare opportunity for visitors and locals to meet and socialize in a convivial atmosphere. Similar activities take place in the villages of Anse la Raye on the west coast and Dennery on the east coast, where the emphasis is on seafood servings, and Vieux Fort in the south. Additionally, JJ's Paradise in Marigot Bay is a great place to party. There is usually a live band on weekends and their 'Seafood Night' on Wednesdays should not be missed. Believe it or not, all night at JJ's is 'happy hour'.

Shopping in Saint Lucia has taken on an air of sophistication in recent times with some new and classy outlets being opened. To start with, there's Gablewoods Mall at Sunny Acres, just outside Castries, built by local realtor Michael Chastanet. Here you will find all the services expected at a fine shopping centre, and then a little more. For instance, there are a bank, post office, butcher's shop and even a medical centre. In the north is JQ's Mall, which is bigger and has even

▼ Hot sauces

more variety. There are large supermarkets all over Castries and in Vieux Fort, the second town located in the south.

Duty-free Pointe Seraphine is located right in the mouth of Castries harbour. This Spanish-style facility comprises several duty-free shops. Be sure to check it out for such items as jewellery, clothing, perfumes and cosmetics, time pieces and crystal. At Rodney Bay in the north, there is also another good shopping arcade with a range of boutiques and restaurants. The latest addition to the island's shopping experience is Place Carenage on the Castries dock, across from Pointe Seraphine, where you can sample local delicacies and shop at the same time.

Gift shops and boutiques are scattered throughout the island, some too at hotels. Imported linens, locally made straw figures and wood carvings, watches, perfumes, china, pottery and cameras, spices and condiments are just some of the bargains you will find in Castries, for example.

There are many places in Saint Lucia where you can see wood carvings and other objects being created right before your eyes. One of the most famous and popular shops is The Bagshaws, near Morne Fortuné, which specializes in hand-printed fabrics of original design. Eudovic's Art Studio, operated by a Saint Lucian master sculptor, offers local wood carvings created in his own carver's village at the back of Morne Fortuné, where bowls, figures and similar items are hewn from fine native mahogany. Although Saint Lucia boasts several outstanding painters, some stand out like Derek Walcott, Dunstan St Omer, Llewellyn Xavier and Cedric George. There are several art galleries like Artsibit in Castries, Alcina's Art Gallery and Studio at

▲ Wooden crafts

Coubaril, Caribbean Art and Antiques at Cap Estate, Caribbean Art Gallery and The Inner Gallery both in Rodney Bay. Craft shops also abound, selling a wide range of products made by local craftspeople as well as imported items. Noah's Arkade deals in articles of beauty and interest gathered from all over the Caribbean area and sold in delightful shops island wide. Pottery and wood carvings are also available at the Castries Market and the Vendors' Arcade on the other side of the street. At the Caribelle Batik Factory on Morne Fortuné you can actually watch the process of batik and tie-dye using the ancient Indonesian dye-resist method.

Sea Island Cotton Shop in Massade, Gros Islet, offers beautiful hand-made original batiks on high quality sea island cotton. Men's and women's clothing and wall-hangings are a speciality.

Caribbean Perfumes, located in the Vigie Cove area, blends a range of distinctive perfumes and colognes for both men and women using fruits, flowers and precious woods.

Y de Lima, in the main shopping centre in Castries, are the great Caribbean jewellers. There you can find superbly crafted gold and silver necklaces and charms, cameras, watches and a wide selection of film and gift items. Dasheene, at Soufriere, has a unique boutique with exceptional local craft items from the Kinnebrew Collaborative's Black Dahlia collection. And talking of local crafts, you should not miss the little village of Choiseul for hand-made items.

Lately, a number of young enterprising Saint Lucians, eager to capitalize on the growth and success of the tourist industry, have gone into business for themselves producing fashion wear, including batik and crochet garments that are becoming increasingly popular with visitors.

Shopping anywhere in Saint Lucia is safe; nevertheless, visitors are advised to be as prudent as they would be anywhere else in the world. Do not be surprised to find vendors on your hotel beach. They usually have an interesting range of items to peddle: wicker, shell necklaces, palm frond hats, and other local hand-made bric-a-brac, not to mention your favourite souvenir tee-shirt.

There are some special Customs regulations in force, pertaining to visitors, which you will probably find useful to know.

Each returning US resident may take back, without duty, articles totalling US$300, providing that the stay abroad has exceeded 48 hours and that the US$300 exemption, or any part of it, has not been used within the preceding 30 days. The US$300 is based on the retail value of the items in the country where they were obtained.

There is no limit to the number of articles you may take back, as long as you pay duty on the amount in excess of the US$300. The duty on purchases in excess of the US$300 exemption is levied on the wholesale price of the items in the country where they were obtained (the customs officer generally subtracts 40 per cent of your retail cost to arrive at the wholesale value).

In addition to the US$300 exemption, each traveller can mail an unlimited number of gifts, valued at $10 each, to friends and relatives back home, provided the addressee does not receive more than one gift parcel in a day.

One quart of liquor is allowed duty-free per person over 21. Substantial savings can be realized when taking back more than one quart because, even with the duty, it works out cheaper than if bought in a US shop with added sales tax, particularly with higher priced brands.

A total amount of 200 cigarettes for personal use can be taken in duty free within your US$300 exemption. Cigars, however, are limited to 100.

Low-duty items are cameras, watches, perfumes, cultured pearls and shoes. A reduction of the duty on clothing, binoculars and watches bought and used during the trip will be considered by Customs. When declaring these items, mention that they were used on the trip and the Customs officer will reduce the duty appropriately

Free of duty are portable typewriters, foreign photographic film, original paintings, drawings and sculptures, foreign language books, 100-year-old antiques, microscopes over $50, coins for collection, electric shavers, loose diamonds, emeralds, cultured pearls, semi-precious stones, imitation gemstones and coral and cameo jewellery.

⑮ Weddings in paradise

Thinking of tying the knot anytime soon? Where else to do so but in 'paradise'! In recent years, Saint Lucia has become the virtual wedding centre of the Caribbean, the choice of couples, old and young, seeking an exotic venue to say the magical words.

As many as 2500 weddings of visitors a year have been held on the island, and such is Saint Lucia's reputation that it has been voted the Caribbean's top wedding and honeymoon destination by international publications like *Caribbean World* magazine, based in the UK. And *Islands Weddings and Honeymoons* magazine chose Saint Lucia to shoot photographs for its 'Bridal Fashions' section.

Weddings and honeymoons now represent a significant part and welcome new niche of the Saint Lucia tourism market, says a top industry official, and as much as 30 per cent of all visitors come either to get married or to enjoy their honeymoon. In fact, several hotels have been going after this sector of the market in a big way and are reaping the rewards. Most of them have employed wedding coordinators who take complete charge of the occasion.

Innovations in the actual marriage ceremony are emerging all the time, some of them outrageously or hilariously funny. Couples have said their 'I dos' at sea, wearing nothing but their bathing suits, some have gone underwater or under a waterfall, and one Scottish gentleman appeared for the grand occasion wearing his kilt. Many couples have tied the knot in the open air at places like Pigeon Island and Diamond Botanical Gardens. Of course, many still do the traditional church wedding with tuxedo, gown and veil, bells, minister of religion and all, but most ceremonies are performed by a Civil Status Officer or Registrar, appointed by the government, who has to be paid by the couple.

The formalities are quite simple. Applications to be married in Saint Lucia must be

◀ White Bougainvillea

made by a local solicitor to the Attorney General or notary who prepares and signs the licence after a two-day residency period on the island. The couple purchases a licence for EC$200 which is ready for delivery in as little as four days. Birth certificates and passports, proof of decree absolute, if divorced, or death certificate of former spouse, if relevant, are also required. Persons under the age of 18 are required to produce a notarized affidavit from their parents.

Hotels usually arrange any other requirements like a bridal bouquet, buttonholes and other floral arrangements, photos, videos, steel band music, wedding cakes – you name it.

So what are you waiting for? If you are planning a wedding with a difference, then Saint Lucia, the 'Helen of the West Indies' is just the place for you, the perfect starting point in your new life. That's a guarantee.

Clos Pen from Hanging Garden

Bibliography

Annius-Lee, Jacintha, *Give Me Some More Sense,* 1979.

Aubertin, Michael, *Neg Maron,* 2001.

Auguste, Joyce, *Oral and Folk Traditions of St Lucia,* 1986.

Branford, Rupert, *Outstanding Sports Personalities of St Lucia,* 2000.

Breen, H.H., *St Lucia: Historical, Statistical, Descriptive,* 1844.

Ellis, Guy, *St Lucia,* 1981.

Gachet, Charles, *A History of the Roman Catholic Church in St Lucia,* 1975.

King, Winville, *A Tribute to Sir Arthur Lewis,* 1985.

Long, Earl G., *The Serpent's Tale,* 1974.

Marcian, Pierre, Jn., *Tipawol Kweyol (Creole Proverbs),* 1998.

Mondesir, Jones, *Annou-di-i An Kweyol,* 1988.

Nicholas, Floreta, *Two Hearts on a River,* 1990.

Norville, Frank, *Folk Dances of St Lucia,* 1989.

Norville, Frank, *Songs of St Lucia,* 1983.

Odlum, George, *Call That George,* 1979.

Reynolds, Anderson, *The Struggle for Survival,* 1999.

Samuel, Kennedy, *Form, Structure and Characterisation in the St Lucian Folk Tale,* 1978.

St Omer, Garth, *A Room on the Hill,* 1968.

St Omer, Garth, *Nor Any Country,* 1969.

St Omer, Garth, *The Lights on the Hill,* 1986.

Taplin, A.E., *The Day Thou Gavest,* 1988.

Also available in the MACMILLAN CARIBBEAN GUIDES SERIES

Anguilla: Tranquil Isle of the Caribbean – Brenda Carty and
   Colville Petty

Antigua and Barbuda: Heart of the Caribbean – Brian Dyde

The Bahamas: Family of Islands – Gail Saunders

Barbados: The Visitors' Guide – F A Hoyos

Belize: Ecotourism in Action – Meb Cutlack

The Islands of Bermuda: Another World – David Raine

Dominica: Isle of Adventure – Lennox Honychurch

Dominican Republic: An Introduction and Guide – James Ferguson

Grenada: Isle of Spice – Norma Sinclair

Jamaica: The Fairest Isle – Philip Sherlock and Barbara Preston

Nevis: Queen of the Caribees – Joyce Gordon

St Kitts: Cradle of the Caribbean – Brian Dyde

St Vincent and the Grenadines – Lesley Sutty

Tobago: An Introduction and Guide – Eaulin Blondel

The Turks and Caicos Islands: Lands of Discovery – Amelia Smithers
   and Anthony Taylor

Other related titles from Macmillan Caribbean

St Lucia: Portrait of an Island – Jenny Palmer

*Searching for Sugar Mills: An Architectural Guide to the Eastern
   Caribbean* – Suzanne Gordon and Anne Hersh